The Season That Was

The Power of Baseball
to Transform Lives
and Develop Character

By

Dr. Michael F. Price

Clear Light Books
Published by Indigo Sea Press
Winston-Salem

Deep Indigo Books
Indigo Sea Press
PO Box 26701
Winston-Salem, NC 27114

For information regarding bulk purchases of this book, digital purchase and special discounts, please contact the publisher at indigoseapress@gmail.com

Cover photograph of 1975 baseball team: (Front row, left to right): Rick Spencer, Gregg DeSantis, Mark Stacy, Ed Dulkowski, Shawn Girty, Rick DeMeo, Steve Zaugg. (Middle row, left to right): Rich Frey, Stan Duplaga, Mark Fabbro, Dave Williams, Tom Lufft, Jon Kertes, and Don Hynes. (Back row, left to right): Coach Watson, Jim Mellinger, Paul Vargo, Rob Schmidt, Gary West, Gary Freshwater, Rick Bonar, and Ray Searage. Players absent from photo: Mike Anthony, Mike Price, and Randy Shepherd.

Cover design by Pan Morelli
Manufactured in the United States of America
ISBN 987-1-63066-512-8

Dedication

Directly or indirectly, several people rightfully deserve my gratitude because they made it possible for my thoughts to make their way to the written word.

Frank Reuter and Dr. David Javersak helped me to understand the rich history behind how West Liberty State College, now West Liberty University, got its start, some of the individuals that contributed to the school's success over the years, and what policies moved the school forward since its humble beginnings in 1837. Frank T. Reuter's book, West Liberty State College: The First 125 Years, supplied the in-depth information that I needed, while Dr. David Javersak's work West Liberty: From Academy to University, A History, provided me with a much-needed framework of who, what, when, and where. In like manner, I am indebted to the West Virginia & Regional History Center for the photographs of early life at West Liberty, the Wheeling Intelligencer/News-Register, and the good folks at West Liberty who over the years have published *The Trumpet*. The photographs added an extra understanding to the subject.

Similarly, there were all those individuals, librarians, sports information people, and school administrators that supplied me with more contemporary sources. Thanks to their efforts, I was led to school newspapers, college yearbooks, and countless articles from regional, state, and local archives. Thank you: *Noah Becker*, Frostburg State University Athletics, Frostburg, MD; *Kelly Britt*, Assistant to the Librarian, Pickett Library, Alderson-Broaddus College, Philippi, WV; *Becky Brouse*, Sports Information Director, West Virginia University Institute of Technology, Beckley, West Virginia; *Laura Carroll*, Archives, Ohio County Public Library, Wheeling, WV; *Viola (Val) Chontos*, Reference Librarian, St. John Paul II Library, Franciscan University, Steubenville, OH; *Richard DelRusso*, Assistant Librarian,

Seminole Community Library, Seminole, FL; *Jessica Eicklin*, Reference Supervisor, Library Associate, WV and Regional History Center, Morgantown, WV; *Emily Ford*, Archives & Collection Management Assistant Library Technician, Louis L. Manderino Library, California State University, California, PA; *Josh Hill*, Sports Information Director, Davis & Elkins College, Elkins, WV; *Brian Howard*, Director of Athletic Communication, Florida A&M University, Tallahassee, FL; *Carlene Jackson*, Institutional Research and Planning, UNC-W, Wilmington, NC; *Jessie Merrell*, Archives Associate, Schwab Memorial Library, Columbus State University, Columbus, GA; *Dallas Suttles*, Digitization and Computer Services, Archives, Odum Library, Valdosta State University, Valdosta, GA; *Yelizaveta (Liza) Zakharova*, Lewis J. Ort Library, Frostburg State University, Frostburg, MD; *Katy Zane*, Librarian and Head of Learning Resources, Elbin Library, West Liberty University, West Liberty, WV.

Likewise, where would an author be without the behind-the-scenes people? Thank you, Dr. Mike Simpson, and the good folks at *Indigo Sea Press* for your continued faith in me. In a business that thrives in novels and fiction books, you still have a place in your heart for nonfiction like personal finance, church stuff, and the Bible. Additionally, Caren Avera and Bill Northrop took time out from their busy schedules to proofread my work and offer their expert guidance. If nothing else, their eye for detail has made me appear to be a better writer than I actually am.

And then there were the players themselves from that '75 team. Their efforts at staying connected with teammates over the past forty-five years made my job a great deal easier when it was time for me to contact the guys from the team. Above all, I want to thank my former teammates for not only the trust but for the privilege of allowing me to tell a little about that special season that seems to have changed so many lives.

Most of all, I want to thank my wife, Betty, for her patience and understanding. Not once did she complain when I would spend time conducting research in West Virginia or hours writing at the library or at home. She is the perfect spouse and friend, and everyone deserves somebody like her in their life. So thank you, Lovey. You remain a daily part of my thoughts and prayers, although we are miles apart physically, emotionally, and mentally.

—Dr. Michael F. Price

Table of Contents

Introduction

"I owe baseball.
Baseball doesn't owe me a damn thing."
(Pete Rose)

If a person were to ask me to define my foray into the life of a student-athlete in the mid-1970s in one phrase, the phrase would be "without a doubt." Never have three-words, and thirteen simple letters, taken on such transformational and life-changing power as they did for me during my time as an undergraduate at West Liberty State College.

Without a doubt, I would not have been able to attend college if it had not been for the admissions office at (then) West Liberty State College taking a chance on a student that had a less-than-stellar academic record in high school. Truth be told, I graduated 110th in a class of 140.

Similarly, there would have been little chance for me to enroll at WLSC in the fall of 1974 if it had not been for the financial help I received from federal grants, loans, and work-study. My mother was a single parent with six children. Her income sources were the meager $95 a month she received from public assistance and the money she earned cleaning houses and ironing other people's clothes. It wasn't until my junior year in high school that she was hired full-time at the local glass factory. My biological father, inmate number 5590, was nowhere to be found since being released from prison a decade earlier.

Without a doubt, I would not have stayed in college if the West Liberty baseball coach at the time, Jim Watson, would have considered my past rather than my potential. I was neither an all-state, all-region, or all-county baseball player in high school, except in the heart and mind of my mother,

Mary Lou. She considered me to be an all-universe selection. Becoming a member of the Hilltopper baseball team meant that for nine-months, I could be a student-athlete. At the same time, I could spend the summer months working at the local aluminum plant earning money for the next academic year.

Without a doubt, I can confidently say that the four-years that I spent as a student-athlete at West Liberty could be looked upon as the happiest and the most influential years of my life. The education I received started me on a path to becoming a lifelong learner; the friendships I developed are still in place even after four decades; and the overall experience of being a part of such a gifted group of athletes has all contributed to the kind of person I am today. In every sense of the word, all I am as a human being, a husband, a father, grandfather, and everything in-between, can be directly related to the transforming power of baseball. Subsequently, the book's title…*The Season That Was: The Power of Baseball to Transform Lives and Develop Character* says it all. In this sense, I would have to agree with former player Pete Rose when he says, "I owe baseball. Baseball doesn't owe me a damn thing." Herein lies the premise behind this book.

Baseball has the power to move people from where they are to where they can, and should, be…emotionally, relationally, and developmentally. When played with commitment and devotion, it can make us better than we ever thought we could be…on and off the field. Above all, the game of baseball has the propensity to build character, promote values, and shape lives. If you don't believe me, go and ask any one of the twenty-four players on the '75 West Liberty baseball team this question: "did being on the '75 team have anything to do with the kind of person you are today?" Nearly all will say yes. More, the words on the pages of this book are written proof of baseball's transformational power on me and several of my teammates.

Organized with a baseball theme, the book takes the nine months of the 1974-75 academic year and places them into innings. For example, the first full month of classes (September 1974) is the first inning. The second inning is October, the third is November, and so on, with the ninth inning being the month of May 1975 and the end of the academic year. Of course, no "game" is complete without a Pre-game, Extra Inning, and The Final Out.

The Pre-game traces the history of West Liberty from its founding in 1837 to the start of the 1974-75 academic year, including the changes that have occurred within the school over the decades. In the Extra Inning, the pages offer insight into some of the lessons that the players on the '75 team have taken with them into life and what has happened to many of these players after they walked off the field for the last time. As for the final chapter, no book is complete with some closing words. The "meat" of the book, Innings One thru Nine, examines what was taking place in the players' lives, including the games, happenings around the school, and outside the gates to the school. Even something as simple as sharing these events has its limitations.

For starters, one will notice that throughout the book, the school is referred to by its former name, West Liberty State College. This is done to further lend a historical perspective that it's the 1974-75 academic year and not sometime in the future. Granted, there may be instances where something may be mentioned that takes place in the future. Still, these occurrences are few and only included to provide additional insight, context, and understanding. While there may be more content in one "inning" than in another, every attempt has been made to present a well-rounded picture of a student-athlete's life. The "latter" innings will undoubtedly contain much more baseball content since that's the book's primary focus.

The primary source of much of the information about the games, including scores, box scores, line-ups, etc., have come from print articles such as newspapers, particularly the West Liberty school newspaper, *The Trumpet*. When possible, all sources have been cited. However, one will notice two things about the articles that appear in the school newspaper. First, the pieces are commonly "behind" in their reporting of the games, and the stories are usually truncated. This is because the school newspaper was only published during the academic year and had limited space on its pages. More importantly, many campus newspapers, including *The Trumpet*, ceased publication as each semester came to a close. This explains why one will see a shift from the school newspaper to local and regional newspapers as a primary source of information in the book. In those situations when the author was supplied with clippings about the game(s) from a teammate and the clipping fails to include the source, an asterisk (*) follows the article. And while countless attempts were made to discover the source of all information, the search was unsuccessful many times. Another source of information comes from the players themselves. Nevertheless, the information being shared is accurate at the time of the book's publication. Only those stories that could be verified were included in the book.

As with any work, there are undoubtedly some unintended typos by the author, and for that, he apologizes. However, all articles are precisely as they appear in the newspaper. This includes, but is not limited to, misspelled words and names, lousy grammar, incorrect punctuation, players referred to by their last names, or players not mentioned at all. To compensate for this, the author has employed two remedies. First, he has chosen to include multiple articles of the same game in many instances in hopes that all players get their fair share of being mentioned. In those situations when a player's name is misspelled, or there is a discrepancy within the article, the author notes the error with a (sic) to convey that he recognizes the incorrect spelling and is admitting it to the reader. One must remember that this book is being written as if it were the 1974/75 academic year. As such, computers with spellcheck were still in the infant stages of development.

Next, it must be mentioned that every attempt has been made to contact each of the twenty-four members of the '75 team to make them aware of the book. Beyond the mailing of letters to the player's last known address, countless attempts have been made through emails, Facebook, and calls using the player's last known phone number. All told, the author has been able to make contact with nearly half of the twenty-three players. One of the players, Rick Bonar, is deceased.

Finally, not only for simplicity but also for keeping a "running tally" of wins and losses during the '75 season, the author has chosen to include an ongoing record of the team's overall and conference record before each game series. Hopefully, this will reduce any confusion over the team's record due to a lapse in time between when the game was actually played and the results' reporting.

––––––––––

Growing up in a small town about 90-minutes to the south of WLSC, I had some knowledge about the school. For one, my oldest brother spent several months there as a student until his number came up in the draft, and he ended up being sent to Vietnam. A second source was my high school baseball coach, a graduate of the school and played on the baseball team years before. My final source of information about the school came from my baseball playing days in high school. WLSC was the designated site for local teams that had advanced to regional level playoffs. These three sources formed the limited depth of my knowledge of the academics and athletics at the school. Who would have ever guessed the school would become my home-away-from-home for four years and the site of some of my best memories of playing college baseball. Like so many of the other students that enrolled in the late summer of 1974, I knew "of" West Liberty, but I really didn't "know" the school.

Pre-game (August 1974)

"Baseball is like church.
Many attend. Few understand."
(Leo Durocher)

Nestled among the rolling hills of northern West Virginia lies one of the hidden treasures of higher education within the state...West Liberty State College. Regardless of the route one travels to get to the school, north on Route 88 from Wheeling, south on Route 67 from Wellsburg, or west along the back roads from West Alexander, Pennsylvania, one will find that the small, rural school is a true diamond-in-the-rough.

For starters, the school is listed annually as one of the leading higher education institutions among small schools in the south. Commonly ranked in the top seventy-five overall, West Liberty regularly finds itself positioned above other southern schools with larger student enrollment. The West Liberty student enrollment typically averages about 2,500 a year.

However, one should not let the size of the school fool you. The small enrollment lends itself to several benefits, including one of the best faculty-to-student ratios in the southern region and in the state, along with reduced class sizes, despite the school drawing students from nearly every one of West Virginia's fifty-five counties, many U.S. states, and several foreign countries. The combination of an acceptance rate of around 70% and a graduation rate of nearly 50% proves that WLSC takes its motto, "To provide our students the opportunity for a high-quality undergraduate, graduate, and professional education," seriously.

7

Equally appealing is the cost to attend West Liberty. Although the in-state tuition rate tends to place the school slightly above the likes of other public state schools such as Glenville State College and Fairmont State University, whose rate falls between $5,100 and $5,500 annually, the cost to attend WLSC currently hovers around $7,800 a year...about $3,900 a semester...or roughly $325/per semester hour. The in-state cost to attend several other state schools such as Concord University, West Virginia State, and the largest school in the state, West Virginia University, can cost as much as an additional $1,000 to $1,500/year. While the out-of-state tuition for students is generally double the in-state rate, the out-of-state tuition rate for those attending WL is less than schools like West Virginia State and WVU, where the price has been known to be as much as three times the in-state rate. As for private colleges and universities within the state, the cost of tuition alone could range as high as $30,000/year.

Similarly, West Liberty has been ranked ahead of some more noted schools for enrolling and graduating disadvantaged students, having one of the safest campuses, some of the best college food, and above-average starting salaries for its graduates. The school is noted for its Business and Dental Hygiene programs. The school has been recognized for its Greek life, fulfilling student life and activities, and "unofficially" ranked as the 3rd best party school among all schools in the state...just behind West Virginia University and Marshall University.

Also, the school has a long-standing tradition of winning sports teams. Over the past two decades, Hilltopper teams, given this nickname because the school sits atop the highest hill in the area, have won WVIAC (West Virginia Intercollegiate Athletic Conference) regular season or conference championships in football (2000, 2009), men's basketball (2010-2013), women's basketball (2000, 2001), men's tennis (2004), women's tennis (2000-2002, 2004, 2006), and women's golf (2010).

But in one sense, West Liberty in 1975 is a mere continuation of its rich past, a past that is older than the state of West Virginia itself!

The college was founded in 1837, a brief, six decades after the American colonies declared their independence from England. Subsequently, the school could be considered older than nearly one-half of all the U.S. states and almost a decade older than the states of Florida and Texas. They were admitted to the union in 1845. However, most striking is that the college is older than the state of West Virginia itself! West Liberty predates the state by over a quarter of a century. As the last state east of the Mississippi River to be admitted to the union, West Virginia officially joined the other thirty-four states on June 20, 1863.

While it's commonly believed that Adam Black and James Curtis were some of the first to set foot in the area, the lands west of the Alleghany Mountains were considered "open territory" in the years following America's independence. Most of the settlers that "laid down roots" were of English, Scots-Irish, or Welsh descent and came through Pennsylvania. Initially, the town that would later take on the name, West Liberty, was known by one of two titles by settlers: Black's Cabin, named after Adam Black, or Short Creek, because of a creek that ran nearby. Legend says that the town later adopted the name West Liberty because the area was the "western" most part of the new nation that one could find "independence" and "liberty." Between 1777 and 1797, the town of West Liberty had become so well-established and possessed such a worthy reputation among settlers that it was the county seat of government for Ohio County, (West) Virginia. In 1783, the town was laid out, and

9

four-years later, it was granted town rights by the Virginia government. Several prominent men in the area were chosen to lay out the best path for settlers in the area to get to the town. It is commonly believed that the route they selected later became Route 88. One of the local government's first acts was to appoint John McCullough as sheriff. It is generally believed that the area's subsequent growth was aided by two projects...one federal and one privately financed.

Construction of the Cumberland Trail, named for the Maryland town where the first national highway begins its westward route, started in the second decade of the 19th century. With the Potomac River's headwaters as a starting point, the road would generally follow a western path toward Pittsburgh along the (then) Pennsylvania and Virginia borders. Towns along the way would include Frostburg, Maryland, and Uniontown, Pennsylvania. On the outskirts of Washington, Pennsylvania, the highway, composed mainly of crushed stone, would then turn due west toward the Ohio River rather than north toward Pittsburgh. By the time the highway reached Wheeling, (West) Virginia, in 1818, the road's name had become known as the National Road because the road would serve as a route for further expansion westward and a trading route between western farming and eastern markets. The road assisted in establishing Wheeling as a critical commercial and trading route in the upper Ohio Valley.

A second project that contributed to bringing settlers to the area around West Liberty was the building of the B & O Railroad, short for the Baltimore & Ohio Railroad. As with the Cumberland Trail/National Road, the railroad's starting point was in Maryland, in this case, Baltimore. While the railroad's route would later expand north from Baltimore into Philadelphia and New York, the original way was toward the west. From Baltimore, the railroad would run through Cumberland, which welcomed the railroad in the early 1840s. In Cumberland, the railroad would then split; one route would go northwest toward Pittsburgh. The other route would go directly west into (then) Virginia. A decade later, the railroad would reach Fairmont, (West) Virginia. Within six months, the tracks had reached the banks of the Ohio River and the town of Wheeling. By the time the railroad had reached the westernmost bounds in the early 1850s, the college that would eventually be named West Liberty was in its fifteenth year of operation.

The events that contributed to shaping the school's rich history from its beginnings in 1837 to 1975 are best understood in terms of six periods.

1837-1850

In the early spring of 1837, the Virginia legislature granted a charter for a private academy to be established in the town of West Liberty, a small cluster of homes located in the northern part of the state. One year after receiving the charter, the school officially began meeting under the direction and in the house of a Presbyterian minister, Rev. Nathan Shotwell, and his wife, Lydia.

Although he was born in Perth Amboy, NJ, in 1806, and she in 1810, it is commonly believed that the family came to the area following the completion of Rev. Shotwell's studies at Western Theological Seminary in Pittsburgh, PA. His first assignment was to the congregation at the First Presbyterian Church in West Liberty. When they arrived, the Shotwells, who had been married less than four-years, were accompanied by their two-year-old son, Samuel Randolph Shotwell, who was born in September 1835. Rev. Shotwell's efforts in founding the school, later named West Liberty Academy, was in response to the growing need to offer educational opportunities for those living in the area.

Dr. Michael F. Price

When classes began in 1838, Rev. Shotwell and Lydia were the faculty, while the townspeople agreed to act as trustees of the school. At the time, Shotwell was in his early thirties, while his wife was in her late twenties. The first class of the future college numbered less than seventy students, and the original curriculum included oil painting, Latin, logic, music, and arithmetic. The average age of the students in the first class was around 15, but some students were as young as 13-years old. Because the students were meeting in the confines of the Shotwell home, a curtain hanging down the middle of the classroom acted to keep the male and female students separated from one another. However, the academy was not the only school established to provide an education for those in the area.

The establishment of Bethany College, located less than 5-miles from West Liberty on Route 88, followed a similar process in its founding. The initial efforts were led by a minister named Alexander Campbell, who migrated from western Pennsylvania and donated land for the college's first buildings. A short, three-years after students began meeting at West Liberty, the Virginia legislature granted Bethany College its charter.

In the latter years of the 1830s, the West Liberty townspeople raised funds to construct a building so the academy could move from the Shotwell home. Between the time construction began on the new building and its completion in 1839, several things happened relative to the Shotwell circle. First, Rev. Shotwell and Lydia welcomed a second son, Alexander Hamilton Shotwell, born in June 1839. Tragically, Lydia passed away seven months later in January 1840, at the age of 30. Lastly, the new building constructed to house the academy burned to the ground in 1841. The combination of insufficient insurance coverage and no public financial backing meant a lack of funds to rebuild.

Consequently, West Liberty citizens appealed to the Virginia legislature, and the body came through with a gift of $5,000. The money allowed the academy to remain open. In a short time, the residents began raising funds to rebuild. With nearly $30,000 collected, construction started on a new building. In the meantime, the academy was forced to return to the Shotwell home to hold classes.

At about the same time that efforts were underway by the townspeople to reconstruct the second academy building, Rev. Shotwell married for a second time. The date was January 1841, and the wife's name was Martha, who was nine years his junior. A few weeks before Christmas 1844, Rev. Shotwell and Martha welcomed the first of their five children, a boy named Randolph Abbott Shotwell. The three years that followed would see Martha Shotwell give birth to two more boys, Melancthon, born in 1845, and Frederick, born in 1847. In August 1849, the Shotwell's welcomed twin girls, Ruth and Susan; however, they survived only one day after being born. Within a month, Martha would also die at the age of 33-years old.

1850-1875

Exactly three years to the day after his second wife's passing, Rev. Shotwell would marry his third wife, Mary. The date was September 23, 1852. Together, Rev. Shotwell and Mary would have two children, Mary, born in 1853, and a son, McCleary, born in August 1855. By the time the second child was born, however, the family had moved to Mifflin, PA, and Rev. Shotwell had taken a new church. Tragedy struck the Shotwell home a third time when Rev. Shotwell's wife, Mary, died several weeks after giving birth to their son, McCleary. At the time of her passing September 1855, Mary was in her mid-40s.

Two decades after the school's founding, the academy's first permanent building was completed in 1857. The two-story structure measured 80 x 50 feet and was named Academy Hall.

Academy leaders determined that the academic calendar would parallel the "off-season" for farming and run from harvest time in mid-September to planting time in late June. As the academy began classes in the fall of 1858, student enrollment numbered nearly 120, with almost three in every four students being male.

Just before Rev. Shotwell departed the Pittsburgh, PA, area in 1858 and moved to Rutherford, NC, he sent his son, Randolph, to a private school near Pittsburgh. The son would remain at the school until his graduation just before the start of the Civil War. The records also show that in 1859 Shotwell married Rebecca Thompson not long after arriving in North Carolina.

The following year, the academy published its first handbook/catalog and laid out the curriculum for the secondary school. First-year (sophomore) male and female students were required to take eight classes, including Penmanship, Intellectual Arithmetic, Geography, and English Grammar. The twelve classes needed in the second year (junior) consisted of Higher Arithmetic, Physical Geography, Natural Philosophy, Latin, Roman History, and Physical Science. At the start of the student's final (senior) year at the academy, males and females were presented a different curriculum. Required to take no less than 20 classes, the male students were taught Algebra, Geometry and Trigonometry, Natural Philosophy, Botany, Zoology, and General History. There were even classes on horses and surveying, made possible by an increase in faculty size. Simultaneously, the mandatory subjects for all females included such disciplines as literature, writing, and geography.

It seems the rules of student conduct were just as structured. Male and female students were not allowed to speak to each other unless they were in a faculty member's presence. There was no dancing, no card playing, or visiting taverns. If caught doing any of these things, the student could face public reprimand. As one might expect, since the school was established by a minister, all students were bound to attend the daily chapel service and public worship each Lord's Day. Many of these rules remained in place until the early years of the 1900s. Most stayed either in private homes in the area or in a nearby boarding house for those students who needed housing.

Col. W.B. Curtis

The American Civil War brought its own challenges to the school. Some within the academy were drawn to side with the federal government. At the same time, others sided with Virginia and advocated secession from the Union. All of this was taking place, even as one resident in the area, William Baker (W.B.) Curtis, who had moved to West Liberty in 1832, was in attendance at an 1861 meeting in Wheeling to discuss the formation of a new state. When President Abraham Lincoln issued a call for an additional 300,000 troops in 1862, Curtis took up the call. He recruited countless students from the academy into what came to be known by many as the Wheeling Home Guard. Training in nearby Wheeling, Curtis' group became Company D of the 12th West Virginia Infantry when West Virginia seceded from Virginia on June 20, 1863. As a result of nearly every male at the academy going off to war, the decline in enrollment caused the academy to go into debt and nearly bankrupted the school. Despite the mounting debt, however, the West Liberty Academy was able to stay open.

In 1866, W.B. Curtis was elected into the West Virginia legislature. Within months of the end of the war, a local committee was formed and headed by Curtis. The plan was to convince the legislature to purchase the school. In 1867, a bill was passed, and the state agreed to buy the academy for the amount of the school's debt, $6,000. However, the school would continue to operate as West Liberty Academy. The school became the official property of the state of West Virginia on March 2, 1870. In addition, the school received a new name…West Liberty State Normal School…along with a new mission. It would become the region's first training school for teachers. Between 1838 and the selection of F. H. Crago in 1870 as the school's first principal following the state's acquisition, the school had seen five principals come-and-go.

The first commencement took place in 1872, exactly thirty-five years after the school's founding. In addition to faculty, the public and fellow students were allowed to ask students questions as part of the senior's oral examinations and graduation. For the next two years, the school would not receive any funds from the West Virginia legislature.

1876-1900

Just as the Reconstruction Era came to a close in 1877, the school's alumni association was founded. The first year of the group's existence saw the size of the membership swell to over 100. It was a good thing because student enrollment seems to have found itself on a downward trend.

In 1873, the student population hovered just shy of 100. The following year, the enrollment had been reduced to fifty-four, and less than 40 at the start of the 1876/77 academic year. The founding of the association may have also helped to relieve some of the school's financial challenges. However, there may be little doubt of W.B. Curtis and his wife's contribution to the school's alumni association's growth. The Curtis' home, known as Liberty House, was a gathering place for students during this time and the site of an annual graduation dinner hosted by W.B. and his wife. The tradition continued until shortly after W.B. Curtis died in 1891.

Remarkedly, the school began a slow but steady increase in enrollment starting in the fall of 1877 when nearly 60 students signed up for classes. By the start of classes in 1879, the number had risen to around 70. Despite the ups-and-downs, one thing remained the same...the academic calendar. Since the academy first began meeting in 1838, the school term would run from the first Monday in September and end the last Wednesday in June of the following year. Besides a two-month break during July and August, the students would have a one-week break for Christmas.

As a result of the school's growing academic reputation and an increase in enrollment, the West Virginia legislature appropriated $8,000 in funds in 1893 to build an addition to Academy Hall. The hall was completed in 1895, but a fire destroyed much of the building in 1896. Thanks to the state legislature, the school secured funds of $3,000. The generous gift allowed the annex to be rebuilt the following year. In that same year of 1896, the school fielded its first sports team, most likely, football.

Naturally, the sizes of the graduating class varied from year to year. One year in the early 1880s, there was only one graduate, while the senior class of 1898 included 9 women and 2 men. For several years in the last quarter of the 1800s, a wagon brought students who lived in Wheeling to the school. It was a 2-hour, one-way ride up Route 88, and the wagon ran several times a week.

For the next six decades, the school would operate as a teacher preparatory institution and a high school. The high school would eventually close after the 1923 academic year.

In 1890, the school received word of the passing of Rev. Shotwell. He died on September 10, 1890, in Rogersville, TN. Rev. Shotwell was 83-years-old.

1900-1925

In the first few years of the 20th century, the school recorded its largest enrollment to date and the largest number of alumni, nearly 300 in 1906. Nevertheless, the size of the faculty at the school the same year numbered less than ten. The school called its first "official" president, John C. Shaw, in 1908. Until that time, those that led the school were called principals. Before coming to West Liberty, Shaw had been

Baseball team, undated

the principal at Glenville Normal School in Glenville, WV, where he had served for the past eight years. Still, Shaw was familiar with the school at West Liberty because he had taught there for four years, beginning in 1897. His presence may have provided a calming element, mostly since West Liberty had seen no less than thirteen principals between 1870 and 1908...an average tenure of fewer than three years for each. It is generally believed that the school's first baseball team took the field just before Shaw arrived in 1908.

One of President Shaw's first acts was to petition the West Virginia legislature in 1910 for a grant so the school could purchase land. When his request was denied, the records convey that Shaw used his own money to purchase nearly fifty acres of land to the south of the school's original location for around $100 an acre. He later bought an additional thirty acres. Seeking to laud the positives of the school, the 1912 catalog stressed the points that the school was in a "...beautiful location (free of malaria and typhoid), small classes, and moderate expenses." (R. Schramm, *West Liberty State College*, 2001, pg. 15).

West Liberty Normal School, 1912

In 1915, the West Virginia legislature approved a gift of $70,000 to the school. In addition to purchasing the original 46 acres of land from Shaw for the amount he had paid for the land, $6,000 plus interest, a women's dorm was to be built on the school's future site. Sometime later, Shaw purchased additional land on behalf of the state. His third purchase brought the total size of the land of the school to about 100 acres. However, the actual construction of the dorm did not begin until 1918.

Between 1906 and the start of World War I, student enrollment averaged nearly two hundred. But just as the Civil War negatively affected the college, the same proved to be the case with World War I. The war drew countless males from the school into the service. The student population at the outset of the 1918/19 school year numbered just over 100. Consequently, the result was an enormous decrease in revenues.

Moreover, there were no football teams fielded between 1919-1923. However, President Shaw did not allow the war to disrupt his plans to move the school forward. While one of his initial acts was to approve a summer schedule of classes so teachers could take additional courses, one of his last before his departure in 1919 was laying the foundation on a three-story, red brick building just inside the entrance to the college. It was also decided that the academic year would be set at two-semesters, and each session would be eighteen weeks.

In 1920, the school hired a new president, Howard J. McGinnis. During his brief five-years or so, he endeavored to follow his predecessor's path and move the college forward…physically, academically, and athletically.

Not long after taking office, McGinnis had the honor of officially welcoming female students to the newest building on campus. Since the women students outnumbered the male students during this time, it was decided that the new dorm would be a female dorm. The dorm, later to be named Shaw Hall in honor of President Shaw, opened in January 1920. However, the addition of the dorm ushered a growing need for more water to the campus. In response, McGinnis directed a dam to be constructed on a nearby creek to provide a direct water source to the new dorm and beyond. Not long after applying to the state legislature for additional funds, McGinnis' request was approved. He used the money to build a library, more classrooms, and a new gymnasium that opened in 1922. By this time, the size of the faculty had grown to over a dozen.

Physical Education Building, 1922

During McGinnis' years as president, West Liberty would initiate the process that would ultimately lead to the school becoming a four-year, degree-granting, teachers' college. In like manner, during his term in office, the school would add physical education to the school's curriculum, begin a school newspaper, and establish a new theater group on campus, the Hilltop Players. While the first newspaper was called *The Normal Trumpet*, the name would hold for nearly seventy-five years, until the name was changed to simply, *The Trumpet*. Equally pertinent to the college's expansion during this time was an event that happened in the latter years of McGinnis' tenure.

In 1924, it was generally believed that West Liberty joined fellow West Virginia schools Alderson-Broaddus College, West Virginia University, Marshall University,

Bethany College, Potomac State College, West Virginia Tech, and Salem College, along with Morehead College (KY) to form the West Virginia Intercollegiate Athletic Conference (WVIAC).

Girls' Gym Class

When it was reported that the school had only graduated around 730 students during its first fifty years of existence or about 15 students per graduating class, state officials took note. The combination of low enrollment, just over 125 at the beginning of the 1925/26 school year, along with a weakening of community support, prompted a discussion by state leaders if the school should be relocated to nearby Wheeling. After much debate, and through McGinnis' tireless efforts, it was decided that the school should remain in its current location. At the time, a common belief was that the building of Shaw Hall and its potential to provide space for additional residential students to attend the school may have contributed to keeping the campus at its present site.

After leaving West Liberty in 1919, President Shaw went on to work for the state of West Virginia until his retirement in 1933.

Following his tenure, Dr. McGinnis became a faculty member at East Carolina University (NC). He was also acting president at the school from 1944-46. Dr. McGinnis passed away in 1971. The McGinnis Theater at ECU is named in his honor.

1926-1950

On July 1, 1926, John S. Bonar, West Liberty Class of '13, became the school's third president. More, he simply picked up where his predecessors left off. One of Bonar's first acts was to expand the dam's size, which sup-plied water to the school, and have a filtration system installed on the water line running to the campus. In 1927, President Bonar took the water system one step further when he directed the school to construct a large water tank on one of the town's highest points. In turn, this supplied water to the town as well as the campus. Even though the reservoir would frequently run out of water, the system significantly improved town and campus conditions.

Bonar also saw to it that electricity reached not only the college's buildings but also the homes of the full-time residents of the town of West Liberty.

President's House

At the same time all this was going on, President Bonar was working diligently to secure funds from the state legislature for new building construction on the expanding campus. Eventually, funds from the legislature of $100,000 were acquired, and construction began. The first building to be constructed would be Curtis Hall, named after the local military hero and college advocate, W.B. Curtis. It was completed in 1929 and followed two years later by the completion of McCollough Hall. While both buildings would be three-stories and match architecturally, Curtis Hall would house classrooms while McCollough Hall, the school's library. Years later, the two buildings would be joined to become the east and west wings of Main Hall. With all the new buildings popping up around the 100-acre site, the people in the area began referring to the president as "Bonar, the Builder." With the completion of Curtis Hall and McCollough Hall, the number of buildings on the new campus grounds now numbered four, including Shaw Hall and the gymnasium.

Main Building and Class of 1927

To add a degree of decorum and respectability to the student body, Bonar expected all male students to wear a coat and tie when eating in the co-ed cafeteria at Shaw Hall.

The athletic programs at West Liberty also benefitted from President Bonar's strong leadership skills. During his years in office, the enrollment nearly quadrupled, which directly affected the school's sports program. Between 1926 and the last year of his tenure, the football and basketball programs had won several conference titles. As expected, the sudden rise of athletic dominance garnered the attention of other schools. The other schools around the state began accusing West Liberty of admitting any male student that

Football team, 1927

would assist the school in its sports programs. Bonar's solution was to institute a four-step process by which male students who wanted to play sports would be admitted. The student-athlete would be accepted if he fell into one of the four categories: were a graduate of a first-class high school, possessed at least 15-hours of high school credit, were a teacher, or if the student was over 21-years old and was capable of handling an average academic load of classes. At about the same time, the school's sports teams were getting a new name. Before Bonar's tenure, the teams went by the nickname of the Liberties or the Normalites. The new name chosen for the school's teams would be the Hilltoppers. By 1928, the school offered three-year college classes for those interested in improving their situation.

In one final act before the end of his tenure in 1930, Bonar approached lawmakers about renaming the school to better reflect its primary mission to train students to become teachers and educators. His tireless efforts came to fruition in

1931 when the state legislature voted to change the school's name from West Liberty Normal School to West Liberty State Teachers College.

Whatever historians may end up writing about President Bonar, there is little doubt that his progressive vision, get-it-done attitude, and deep devotion to his alma mater will not, and should not, ever be forgotten.

Baseball team, 1927

Between Bonar's departure in 1930 and 1935, the Great Depression's adverse effects seemed nominal to the school. The entering freshman class of 1933 numbered less than 200. As before, the declining enrollment meant a decline in revenues. In turn, this meant not only a reduction in faculty and staff but some slowdown in the school's plan to grow and expand. However, the consequences of the Depression upon the college was about to change with the calling of Dr. Paul Elbin as the school's president in 1935. Within weeks of Elbin taking office on August 13, he began utilizing many of the federal government's Depression-era relief programs to benefit the college.

In 1936, Elbin used funds from the Works Progress Administration and the Public Works Administration to construct a new dormitory for men. Completed in 1937, the dorm was initially called Fraternity Hall but was later changed to Shotwell Hall to honor the school's founder, Rev. Nathan Shotwell. As one of the first buildings a person would see as they entered the main gate to the campus, the dorm was a sight to see. The two-story, red-brick structure had nearly fifty rooms, but the rooms were smaller than the rooms' size in the other dorm on campus, Shaw Hall. There was space for twin beds in Shaw Hall, while the size of the places in Shotwell would accommodate only bunk beds.

Similar funds were used to build the first Student Union in the state, improve nearby roads, and update the school's sports facilities. As well, Elbin began weekly programs over Wheeling radio station WWVA.

In 1937, Elbin introduced a radio show called Bible Question Bee. As part of the weekly program, the host would include students from the college and local kids from around the area and ask them Bible-related questions. President Elbin acted as a modern-day Alex Trebek.

The following year, the college began offering business courses, a two-year program in secretarial studies, and a four-year degree in business education. In addition, the school's dental hygiene program was established, one of the earliest such programs in the nation. Two years later, the school would graduate its first class. Most progressive, West Liberty opened a downtown campus in nearby Wheeling. The classes were held at Wheeling High School. Above all, Elbin directed the downtown campus to admit African-Americans as part of its open enrollment policy. Included in the list of epic events of the year was the news the school had been waiting on, namely, the school's unconditional accreditation from the West Virginia Board of Regents.

The outbreak of World War II brought the grim reality of a decrease in student enrollment, especially among males. Between the war years of 1941 and 1945, the overall student population fell from nearly three hundred full-time students at the onset of the war to just over 200 in 1943. And while there may have been less than 100 students on campus when the war came to a close in 1945, less than ten were males.

Moreover, the decline in student enrollment created a ripple effect across the entire campus. Sports programs were canceled, the publication of *The Trumpet* scratched, and Shotwell Hall, the dorm built especially for male residents attending the school, was temporarily closed.

About the time that Gen. George Patton was leading his tank troops to victory in Tunisia, the school received word from the state legislature that the school's request to change the school's name, the second name change in less than fifteen years, had been granted. To better reflect the college's evolution from being a teacher's college to one that now offered courses in business, the liberal arts, and the higher professions, henceforth, the school would be referred to as West Liberty State College.

As the fall semester began in 1945, the student enrollment had nearly reached pre-war numbers. The following year saw the school enrollment reach its highest number to date, and upwards of two-thirds of the students were males. The driving force in this rise in student population was the introduction of the G.I. Bill. In 1946, the college fielded its first football team after four years of having no team. Between 1947-50, the football team would produce a 41-3-3 record, including two winning streaks. The first was 24 straight games followed by a streak of 19 consecutive games without a loss.

To manage the increase in enrollment and the challenges this placed on the school's physical plant, the school purchased an additional 100 acres of land in 1948, which raised its total size to nearly 300 acres.

As the school readied itself to begin the 1950/51 academic year, it sought to pay homage to the leadership of former President John S. Bonar, who passed away a decade earlier and is buried near the campus. A headstone marks the site of his grave. On one side of the monument are the words "West Liberty State Normal School 1926-31" and "Curtis Hall." On the other side of the stone is the phrase "West Liberty State Teachers College" and "McCollough Hall."

1950-1974

Enrollments leveled off in the early 1950s, then rose again by the mid-decade, as GIs from the Korean conflict took their places in West Liberty classrooms. Moreover, the Elbin Revolution continued with several firsts. New programs were added in art, music, and home economics. The school hired its first professor of speech and the first dean of students. In addition, the school called its first trained librarian and first dietician. Last but not least, President Elbin played a significant role in reviving the school's theatrical group, the Hilltop Players, and establishing a Faculty Club.

The increase in school programs seems to have led to a rise in student enrollment. During the decade of the 1950s, the student population at the school averaged nearly 1,500 a year…a whopping 75% increase over enrollment numbers of the previous decade. As part of the changing dynamics in the student population, male freshmen were required to wear a "beanie" and sing the school's alma mater upon the demand of an upperclassman. Freshmen were even required to wear the "beanie" in the shower and in bed. Veterans objected to the practice and were declared exempt.

As expected, the increase in student population brought a flurry of new building construction. First, it was Rogers Hall in 1959, followed by the completion of Main Hall joining (old) Curtis Hall and McCollough Library in 1960. Between 1964 and 1968, there were no less than five new dorms built, including Bonar Hall, Curtis Hall, Boyd Hall, Bartell Hall, and Hughes Hall. Each hall is named in honor of an individual connected to the school.

Rogers Hall was named for Clara West Rogers, Dean of Women, between 1937-1952. As expected, Bonar Hall is named for John S. Bonar, who presided over the school from 1926 to 1933. Curtis Hall is named in honor of General William B. (W.B.) Curtis and his family. Boyd Hall bears the name Mrs. Robert Lee Boyd of Wheeling to recognize her services as a State Board of Education member. Bartell Hall is named after Dr. Joe Bartell, former dean of students and athletic director. Hughes Hall was named for Raymond G. Hughes, a member of the English faculty from 1931 until 1970. The Hall of Fine Arts, the Interfaith Chapel, a remodeled and enlarged College Union, and the Paul N. Elbin Library followed between 1966 and 1970.

The decade of the 1960s also brought other changes. In 1963, a mascot was chosen for the school…a black bear named "Topper." The following year the school's baseball team won a national title. In 1966, the school welcomed the addition of fraternities and sororities to the college community. That same year, the sports teams' colors changed from black and orange to black and gold.

Before Dr. Elbin retired in 1970, and his position as president of the college was filled by Dr. James Chapman, student enrollment had reached over 3,500. However, the excitement was short-lived. The following year, the state Board of Regents forced the school to give up its Wheeling campus to establish a new college, West Virginia Northern Community College. Between 1972 and 1974, the campus landscape continued to change. With the introduction of Title IX to the sports programs in 1972, the number of women's sports at the school increased from the traditional ones of field hockey, tennis, softball, and basketball. September 5 of that year brought another change when the pub opened for the first time. Hours were Monday-Friday, 6:00pm to 12:00

midnight. On Fridays and Saturdays, the opening was at 1:00pm and closed twelve hours later. Also, in 1972, the Education Department at the school set down a dress code for student teachers. Girls were forbidden to wear a skirt or dress whose hemline was above the knees, and excessive eye makeup. Most notably, all female student teachers had to wear a bra and a girdle. As for male student teachers, they were not allowed to have sideburns below the ear or have a mustache. Finally, all prospective male teachers had to wear jockey shorts rather than boxers.

Just in time for the start of the 1974-75 academic year, Krise Hall, the newest of the dorms, opened its doors for student housing.

While the country was cloaked in shock from the Watergate break-in and the subsequent resignation of President Richard Nixon weeks earlier, the opening of the 1974-75 academic year in August brought newness for first-year students and a restart for returning students. The dorms opened up on Sunday, August 25, and most students began arriving on the same day.

Beyond the widespread presence of polyester, bright colors, and loose-fitting clothes, female students wore T-shirts, jeans, khakis, bellbottoms, hip-huggers, and seer-sucker culottes. For the guys, it was white painter's pants, red flannel shirts, and cut-off shorts. Students had spent the summer watching educational shows like *60 Minutes*, *Face the Nation,* and *Captain Kangaroo*. They talked about the latest episode of *All in the Family*, or the hilarious clips from *Candid Camera* and *The Benny Hill Show*. And some wanted to know the newest from *All My Children*, *Days of Our Lives*, *As the World Turns*, and *General Hospital*. However, the biggest question circulating among most of the male students was that week's game on *Monday Night Football*. In contrast, the most significant inquiry among most of the

Dr. Michael F. Price

female students revolved around the new movie, *The Longest Yard,* starring Burt Reynolds.

Lastly, it seems that familiar phrases were running rampant around the campus, and included, "My bologna has a first name, it's O-S-C-A-R"…"Correctamundo"…and "Keep your friends close, but your enemies closer."

Tuition and fees for the 1974/75 academic year hovered around $150 per semester hour or approximately $1,800 for those students taking 12-hours or more. The tuition rate was roughly four times that rate or $600 per semester hour for out-of-state students. The student that stayed on campus would expect to pay around $600 a semester for room and board. All told, a student entering WLSC in the fall of 1974 should expect to pay no less than $2,400 per semester or just shy of $5,000 for tuition, fees, room, and board for the year.

Although the nearly 300-acre setting may have seemed daunting to new students, the West Liberty campus was easily navigated. At opposite ends of the campus was Bartell Hall to the south and Hughes Hall to the north. Bartell Hall is a male dormitory and houses predominantly upperclassmen. Hughes Hall is located next to the baseball field and is an all-female dorm. Upon departing Bartell Hall, students could either walk up the hill to get to the central part of campus or walk north and west, make their way past Krise Hall, and then to the main campus. Krise Hall is a co-ed dorm and home to one of the two on-campus cafeterias. Continuing past Krise Hall, a student will then find themselves in front of two dorms that sit adjacent to each other, Bonar Hall and then Curtis Hall. Bonar Hall houses principally male, freshman students. Like its counterpart to the north, Curtis Hall is also a freshman dorm and primarily houses male students. A short walk directly east from Bonar and Curtis

Hall will find a student in the heart of the campus, the Quadrangle.

Laid out in the traditional college design, the Quadrangle is bordered on all sides by buildings. Looking west, a student finds Shotwell Hall. Next to Shotwell Hall to the south is the Interfaith Chapel. Looking due south, a student will see the Fine Arts Building, which is the site for music classes, theater productions, and concerts.

As one looks to the south and east, a student will see Arnett Hall, where the science classes are taught. The building is named for Denver Arnett, who held the post of academic dean at West Liberty from 1955-1970. Due north of Arnett Hall is the Student Union. Here, students will find the bookstore, the location for weekly movies, and, most importantly, the pub.

To the immediate north of the Quadrangle is the Main Hall. Housed within its walls are mostly class and administrative offices of the school, including the Business Office, the Office of Financial Aid, and the office of the college president, Dr. James Chapman.

Just outside the main walkways of the Quadrangle to the south and east is the Health and Physical Education Building. In addition to some classrooms, a student will find the large and small gymnasiums, the school's swimming pool, and locker rooms. A few steps to the north is Boyd Hall, an all-female dorm. And just north of Boyd Hall is Rogers Hall, the location of the school's other cafeteria.

The remaining buildings on campus are Shaw Hall and the Paul Elbin Library. Elbin was not only the longest-tenured president in the school's history serving from 1935-1970 but was the youngest college president in the nation when he was chosen for the position. President Elbin was 30-years old when he first took office.

Dr. Michael F. Price

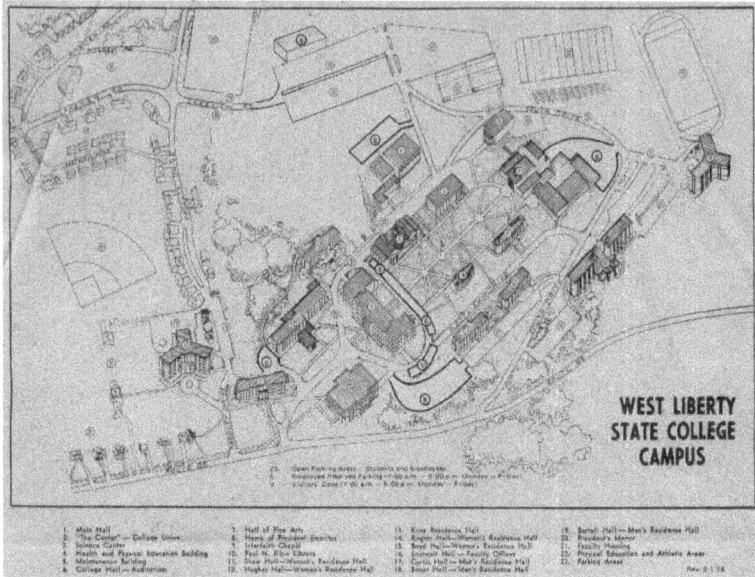

WEST LIBERTY
STATE COLLEGE
CAMPUS

The fall semester officially began on Tuesday, August 27, 19074, with several night classes. The list included Business Law I, Cases in Marketing Strategy, Corporate Finance, Fundamentals of Guitar, History of Social Thought, Human Development I, Managerial Accounting, Marriage and Family, Music History I, Oral Interpretation (Speech), Psychology of Childhood and Adolescence, State and Local Government, and Topics in American Literature.

While it may have been difficult for those that had a class that first night, the weather may have made it doubly challenging to concentrate. When night classes began at 6:00pm, the temperature was a pleasant 79 degrees and a mild 68 degrees when classes let out at 10:00pm. At 8:00am the next day, the first full day of classes, the temperature was a chilly 58 degrees. By the time the last of the day classes were dismissed around 4:00pm, the temperature had risen some 22 degrees to an encouraging 80 degrees.

With an elevation of 1,224 feet above sea level, it came as no surprise to anyone that the school's athletic teams' nickname would be the Hilltoppers. There would be Hilltopper football, soccer, cross-country, basketball, swimming, and wrestling on the men's side of sports in the fall season alone. On the women's side, there would be Hilltopper tennis, field hockey, and volleyball. But for those in the know, the most recognizable and lauded of the school's teams at the time was Hilltopper baseball.

The records indicate that the West Liberty baseball team did not win a single conference title between 1947 and 1962. During those sixteen years, Fairmont State College won the title 4 times; Morris Harvey College three times; Concord College, West Virginia State, Salem College, and West Virginia Wesleyan; each won the trophy twice. West Virginia Tech won the crown in 1947, while Salem and Morris Harvey split the prize cup in 1949. But the tide would change for 'Topper baseball beginning with the 1962 season.

In the decade between 1962-1971, the Hilltopper baseball team would average over 17 wins a year against 8 losses overall. In the WVIAC, the team would average 9 wins a year and 2 losses. During one three-year span, the team did not lose a single conference game! Most impressive, the team won a national championship in 1964. Leading the team during those years was Coach George Kovalik, who coached from 1962-1964, followed by Tom Meikle from 1965-1967, then Dave Waples for two-years beginning in 1968. For two seasons, 1970 and 1971, the 'Topper baseball team was coached by Charlie Campanizzi. At the same time, the Hilltopper baseball team would win four conference

Coach Jim Watson

championships, including three straight between the 1963 and 1965 seasons. Although the school would hire a new coach, the fifth in the span of 10-years, the winning tradition in Hilltopper baseball would continue under the newly appointed Coach Jim Watson.

In his first season (1972), Coach Watson's team would post an overall record of 19-8, 11-2 in the conference, and win the first of his 3-straight WVIAC Northern Division crowns. Not bad for a coach that was working double-duty as the head athletic trainer for the school's sports programs. But while his first team may not have won the WVIAC baseball title that year, a foundation of winning championships and producing players with character had been set in motion.

The following year, Watson's team would go 15-6, win a second Northern Division championship, add the school's first WVIAC baseball title in four years along with a trip to the NAIA Area 7 playoffs. Coach Watson's '74 team would go 14-7 overall, 11-4 in the conference, win his second conference title in a row, and participate in the NAIA Area 7 playoffs.

Inning 1 (September 1974)

If a guy hits .300 every year,
what does he have to look forward to?
I always tried to stay around .190
with three or four rbis,
and I tried to get them all in September.
That way I always had something to talk about
during winter.
(Bob Uecker)

Not long after students began returning from the Labor Day break, fall ball began with high expectations following the highly successful '74 baseball season.

For beginners, the players from the previous year's team contributed to WLSC winning the West Virginia Inter-collegiate Athletic Conference (WVIAC) Commissioner's Cup for the third time in four years. The cup, awarded annually to the school whose athletic teams posted the best overall record among the conference varsity sports, including basketball, bowling, cross country, football, golf, soccer, swimming, and wrestling, was raised when the track, tennis, and baseball teams all won conference championships. Subsequently, all three teams...tennis, track, and baseball...went on to post-season play. The tennis team participated in the National Association of Intercollegiate (NAIA) college tennis championships in Kansas City, MO, where they would end the year tied for 26th in the nation among small schools. After winning the conference crown, several of the men's track team would represent WLSC at the NAIA national track meet in Arkansas. After defeating Morris Harvey College in the finals of the WVIAC championships, the baseball team went on to participate in the Area 7 tournament in Greenwood, South Carolina, where the team finished in fourth place.

Commissioner's Cup: Coach Watson standing, third from right

Similarly, there was a good feeling when fall practice began because of the team's strong performance the previous year. Overall, the team would finish the '74 regular season 14-7 and 11-4 in the conference. Among the non-conference losses would be a 4-0 shut-out at the hands of West Virginia University, a 4-1 loss to Shepherd College, and a 6-2 loss to California State College. Conference losses were to Morris Harvey College 3-1, a shut-out by Alderson-Broaddus 2-0, and two, one-run losses to West Virginia Wesleyan, 3-2 and 9-8. Of the seven losses, two would be one-run and two losses by two-runs. The fourteen Hilltopper victories would include four shut-outs and four one-run games. In total, the '74 team would outscore their regular-season opponents 116-61, an average of over 5 runs a game. In 4 games alone...two against Concord and one each against West Virginia State and Fairmont State College...the team would score forty-four runs.

In like manner, the optimism was high because of the players who would be returning from the '74 team. There were eleven returning players from the previous year's team, including pitchers Mike Anthony, Rick Bonar, Ed Dulkoski, and Dave Williams. Combined, these four individuals had pitched over 164 innings, recorded over 150 strikeouts, and allow less than two-runs a game. Gregg DeSantis, Shawn Girty, Donnie Hynes, Jon Kertes, Jim Mellinger, Robbie Schmidt, and Randy Shepherd would both outhit and outscore their opponents by nearly 2-to-1 and have a combined batting average of over .300. Of these, Kertes was chosen on the WVIAC All-Conference team. Five were All-Conference Honorable Mention...Gregg DeSantis, Jim Mellinger, Shawn Girty, Robbie Schmidt, and Dave Williams...and for a good reason. Kertes hit .420 with 20 RBI's, DeSantis .320, Girty .308, Mellinger .270, and Schmidt .348. As for Williams, his '74 stats included an 8-2 record, an ERA of 1.10, 60 strikeouts in 57 innings, and a no-hitter against West Virginia Tech. The only player gone from the previous year was a three-time All-Conference pitcher, Steve Wojcik, who had signed a contract with the New York Mets.

Clearly, to make the '75 team was not going to be easy for those fifty-or-so players trying out, mainly because there were only twenty-four uniforms. In simplest terms: 24 players on the team, of which eleven were returning, meant there were only thirteen spots left on the roster to be filled. That's if all twenty-four uniforms were given out! The odds of making the team were daunting...three out of every four players trying out would be sent home packing...only 25% would survive the cut and make the team!

―――――――――

With several weeks of try-outs, practices, and intra-squad games now behind them, there remained only two more opportunities for a player to demonstrate his ability and earn a spot on the coming season's roster. The first would be a single, nine-inning game on Sunday, September 29, against players from the Warwood Reds, a local, semi-pro team in the United Mineworkers League. On Sunday, October 6, players "on the bubble" would get one last chance to make their case in a doubleheader with in-state rival, West Virginia University.

The line-up for the single, nine-inning game with Warwood included a mix of veterans Shawn Girty, Jon Kertes, Gregg DeSantis, and Jim Mellinger, along with potential roster players Gary West, Mark Stacy, Rick DeMeo, Stan Duplaga, Tom Lufft, Mike Price, Paul Vargo, and Steve Zaugg. Freshman Ray Searage was the starting pitcher for the 'Toppers. The Hilltoppers beat the Reds by a score of 5-4, with West Liberty scoring three runs in the first inning, and lone runs in the fourth and fifth innings. The holdovers from the '74 team would go a combined 1-16, score one run, collect five walks, with two strikeouts. Senior Jon Kertes would get the lone hit. The remaining players in the lineup that day would go 8-21, scoring four runs, five RBI's, including Steve Zaugg's triple. While Ray Searage started the game, fellow freshman Mark Fabbro would pitch the last three innings, giving up four hits, recording two strikeouts, and allowing one earned run.

An article appearing in the *Wheeling News-Register* on October 6 entitled "W. Liberty, WVU Meet In Baseball Games," reports…

Concluding fall workouts, West Liberty State College's baseball team meets West Virginia University in a doubleheader today starting at 1 p.m. on the Hilltoppers' diamond. Head Coach Jim Watson plans to take a look at returning pitching veterans Dave Williams and Mike Anthony in the seven-inning contests, along

*with at least four other prospects. Watson also
intends to use most of the players on his roster
in the fall final outing. Last Sunday, the
Hilltoppers gained a 5-4 victory in an exhibition
game against the Warwood Reds' sandlot team.
Promising freshman prospect Ray Searage
hurled three and two-thirds innings, striking out
six, and giving up just one earned run...Stan
Duplaga slammed a triple while Gary West and
Tom Lufft each had two hits for the winner.*

In like manner, an article appearing in *The Trumpet* on
October 23, entitled "Hilltoppers Split Final Doubleheader,"
summarized the game with the Warwood Reds by saying…

*...a nine-hit attack led by Gary West and Tom
Lufft with two hits apiece. West Liberty moved
ahead 3-1 in the first inning when Stacey (sic)
reached second on a throwing error and West,
designated hitter, doubled to drive in the first
run. Kertes walked and freshman Stan Duplaga
tripled to center, scoring West and Kertes.
Warwood tallied runs in the fourth and fifth, but
West Liberty countered in both as West got his
second RBI with a single, and with 2 out in the
fifth, Steve Zaugg tripled in the deciding run.*

———————

As for the doubleheader with West Virginia University,
The Trumpet of October 23 reports on the first game by
saying…

*...A home run by Jon Kertes highlighted the
scoring for the Hilltoppers in the opener, as
West Liberty won 4-3. Kertes paced the team with
two hits and two RBI's. Greg (sic) DeSantis and
Tom Lufft added doubles and Stan Duplaga and
DeSantis had RBI's. Dave Williams went all the*

41

*way for the Hilltoppers, striking out 8 and
giving up only one earned run.*

And for the second game…
*…Mike Anthony's five shut-out innings in the
second game gave the Hilltoppers a chance to
run up a 5-0 lead before bowing 7-6 in 10
innings. Outfielders Shawn Girty and Mike Price
combined efforts to collect half of the total team
hits as West Liberty out-hit WVU 12-7. Girty led
off the 3-run first inning with a single to right,
added a bunt in the second and a double in the
eighth as he reached base safely four times,
scored twice and had a stolen base to his credit.
Price was 3-4 and second baseman Mark Stacy
contributed 2 hits. Sophomore Ed Dulkoski was
tagged with the loss, although he turned in an
excellent performance, retiring 11 straight in the
final four innings…*

Similarly, in a lengthy article that appeared not long after
the close of fall ball, the piece relates the following about the
games with West Virginia University…
*West Liberty State baseball team completed fall
workouts on Saturday by dividing a doubleheader
with invading West Virginia University. The
Hilltoppers won the opener, 4-3, behind the five-
hit pitching of Dave Williams, who struck out
eight and walked three. A two-run homer by Jon
Kertes in the third inning provided the winning
runs. Kertes went two for two in the opener,
while Greg (sic) DeSantis had two hits and
freshman Tom Luff slammed a double. In the
second game, the hosts shot to an early 5-0 lead
behind Mike Anthony but relievers…had control*

*problems which permitted the Mountaineers to
tie it up. Out of the bullpen came Ed Dulkoski,
who pitched five strong innings of relief, yielding
only two hits but winding up a hard luck 7-6
loser on an unearned run in the 10th inning.
Shawn Girty and Mike Price had three hits each
in the second game while Mark Stacy, returning
after missing last season with an illness,
pounded out two hits. Head Coach Jim Watson
was pleased with the defensive work on his team.
"We turned in four double plays and our work in
the field most of the day was very good," he said.
The busy Hilltopper coach, who is also head
athletic trainer for all sports, will return his
squad to the practice field in February to
prepare for the spring southern junket in early
March...* *

But while change seems to be in the air surrounding
Hilltopper baseball, there is one constant on the
field...Coach Jim Watson.

Entering the '75 season, Watson's three-year record
stands at a remarkable 45-22 overall...a .681 winning
percentage. More impressive, however, is Watson's
conference record during those same three seasons. The 37-
11 record equates to an astounding .770 winning percentage.

Equally impressive is the way Watson has worked to
bring out the best in his players. Between 1972-74 seasons,
several of Watson's players would be near the top among
conference programs in batting average and stolen bases.
Likewise, the 'Topper pitchers would be annually ranked
among the conference best in strikeouts and the lowest ERA.

Strange as it sounds, the first full month of the school
year was not all baseball for those wanting to see their name

appear on the coming season's roster. Beyond their school work, the players could sneak-a-peak at the Associated Women's Students, all-girl swim party at the campus pool on September 4, attend the concert by the Plum Creek Chamber Ensemble on September 11, or attend Sunday evening worship services in the chapel. For others, one could cheer

Frenchy on the left.

on Dr. Art Barbeau's men's soccer team at their Wednesday, September 18, game against Fairmont State College. At the game, the team would be using new soccer nets for the first time, which meant they could put away the lawn chairs the group had been using as a goal. In addition to the movie *High Plains Drifter*, starring Clint Eastwood, showing at the Student Union on Saturday, September 21, one could attend a women's tennis match or field hockey game during the month. More, one could watch the football team play its home opener versus West Virginia Wesleyan on Saturday, September 28, or the opportunity to bowl unlimited games at the school's bowling alley for a meager $30.00 a semester. Among the over 500 male students signed up to play intramural softball was Hilltopper pitcher, Gary Freshwater, who collected two hits during his fraternity, Theta Xi's, 20-6 whitewashing of the Delta Sigma Pi fraternity. If watching tv in one's room was more of a student's definition of fun, the list of shows included *Chico and the Man*, *Little House on the Prairie*, or the newest show on tv, the recently-debuted *$25,000 Pyramid*, starring Dick Clark. For those whose only desire was to return home after a long day of classes and baseball practice, there was the option of either driving home or hopping on the bus that ran daily between the campus and Wheeling.

Dr. Michael F. Price

Inning 2 (October 1974)

"Well then who's on first?
Yes.
I mean the fellow's name.
Who.
The guy on first.
Who..."
(Abbott and Costello)

A sports guide came out shortly after the 74-75 roster was announced and included biographical information on each player and Coach Watson's evaluation of the player's skill and expected contribution to the team.

Anthony, Michael J. – Junior, 5'9", 160, pitcher, Wheeling, WV. 21-year old Economics major. "He's under-rated, throws two excellent pitches, will see a great deal of mound time."

Bonar, Richard (Rick) – Sophomore, 6'2", 177, pitcher, Hannibal, Ohio. 20-year old Mathematics major and Physics minor. "Shows decisive improvement, with continued motivation will be a pleasant surprise."

DeMeo, Richard (Rick) Charles – Freshman, 5'9", 148, outfielder, Pittsburgh, PA. 18-year old Business Administration major. "Reliable, all-around ball player."

DeSantis, Gregg Anthony – Sophomore, 5'9", 175, catcher, Follansbee, WV. 19-year old Speech major and Business minor. "Great speed, good leader. Solid player in his position."

Dulkoski, Edward (Ed) Alan – Sophomore, 5'9", 160, pitcher, Cadiz, OH. 19-year old Physical Education major. "Developed new pitch in the offseason which will make him a tough competitor."

Duplaga, Stanley (Stan) Timothy – Freshman, 5' 10", 165, third baseman, Wheeling, WV. 20-year-old Marketing major. "Outstanding glove and arm, potential power hitter."

Fabbro, Mark Mario – Freshman, 5'11", 185, pitcher, Newell, WV. 18-year old Accounting major. "Outstanding high school credentials, very live arm."

Freshwater, Gary Charles – Junior, 6'3", 204, pitcher, Colliers, WV. 21-year old Business Marketing major. "Great smoke, best shape of his career."

Frey, Richard (Rich) G. – Freshman, 5'10", 165, shortstop, Pittsburgh, PA. 18-year old Business Administration major. "Versatile utility infielder, excellent arm."

Girty, Shawn Kevin – Sophomore, 5'8', 145, outfielder, St. Clairsville, OH. 20-year old Physical Education major. "Top base stealer in WVIAC, fine all-around player."

Hynes, Donald (Donnie) L. – Sophomore, 5'11', 170, outfielder, St. Clairsville, OH. 20-year old Business Management major. "Good line drive hitter, should show improvement."

Kertes, Jon Paul – Senior, 6'0", 185, outfielder, Germano, OH. 21-year old Physical Education major. "Outstanding power, fine speed, captain, pro-prospect."

Lufft, Thomas (Tommie) Allen – Freshman, 6'1", 165, shortstop, Wheeling, WV. 18-year old Physical Education major and history minor. "Great range at short stop, quick bat and good speed."

Mellinger, James (Jim) Edward – Junior, 6'0", 190, outfielder, Jewett, OH. 21-year old Physical Education major. "Shows improvement each year, can hit long ball, much expected of him."

Price, Michael (Mike) F. – Freshman, 5'10", 160, outfielder, New Martinsville, WV. 20-year old History major and Spanish minor. "Good speed, fine defensive outfielder, transfer from Miami-Dade."

Schmidt, Robert (Robbie) R. – Senior, 6'1", 175, first basemen, Wheeling, WV. 21-year old General Business major. "Premiere defensive first baseman, should have outstanding year at the plate."

Searage, Raymond (Ray) Mark – Freshman, 6'0", 180, pitcher, Deer Park, NY. 19-year old Physical Education major. "Outstanding prospect, could be regular."

Shepherd, Randy – Junior, 5'10", 180, catcher, Cambridge, OH. 20-year old Physical Education major. "Transfer from Austin-Peay, two-year letterman."

Spencer, Richard (Rick) Alan – Sophomore, 5'8", 174, catcher, Steubenville, OH. 21-year old Physical Education major. "First year, good speed, arm, and bat, versatile."

Stacy, Mark David – Freshman, 5'9", 165, second baseman, Steubenville, OH. 20-year old Management major. "Great pivot on double play, extremely reliable."

Vargo, Paul – Freshman, 6'0", 175, first baseman, Benwood, WV. 18-year old Accounting major. "Left-handed hitter with potential to hit long ball."

West, Gary S. – Senior, 6'3", 204, pitcher, Wheeling, WV. 24-year old Biology and Physical Education major. "Returns from service, outstanding hitter with good speed, should be great designated hitter."

Williams, David (Dave) James – Senior, 6'0", 185, pitcher, Coshocton, OH. 22-year old General Business major and Psychology minor. "Drafted by the New York Mets out of high school, fifth in NAIA last year with 1.10 ERA, be premiere in the WVIAC this year."

Zaugg, Stephen (Steve) Richard – Freshman, 5'9", 165, first baseman, Coshocton, OH. 18-year-old Business major. "Good defensive player, swings quick bat."

———————

A quick scan reveals several interesting facts surrounding the new roster of players. Of the twenty-four players, nearly 90% of the team were underclassmen, including ten freshman, six sophomores, and five juniors…Jon Kertes, Robbie Schmidt, and Dave Williams were the only seniors. The list of ten freshmen consists of two pitchers (Fabbro, Searage), six infielders (Duplaga, Frey, Lufft, Stacy, Vargo, Zaugg), and two outfielders (DeMeo, Price). Except for two players from the state of Pennsylvania (DeMeo and Frey) and one from New York (Searage), the remaining twenty-one players are nearly equally divided, with eleven from Ohio and ten from West Virginia. The new roster includes nine players under the age of twenty, of which seven were 18-years old…average age of the players on the team…19.8 years old. Finally, nine of the twenty-four players are majoring in the area of Business, eight in Physical Education, and two in Accounting. The remaining list of majors includes Biology, Economics, History, Mathematics, and Speech.

Many of the players on the '75 roster had played several sports during their high school days. Stan Duplaga, Jon Kertes, and Paul Vargo played baseball, basketball, football, and track; Rick Bonar, Rich Frey, Jim Mellinger, and Steve Zaugg played baseball, basketball, and football; Gregg DeSantis and Gary Freshwater played baseball, football, and ran track; Rick Spencer played baseball, football, and wrestled; Tom Lufft played baseball and basketball. Moreover, many of these same players received honors for their play. Ed Dulkoski was All-OVAC (Ohio Valley Athletic Conference) Special Honorable Mention while playing on the Buckeye West basketball team in 1973. Likewise, Stan Duplaga was an All-OVAC first-team running back selection his junior year at Linsly Institute in Wheeling and a first-team cornerback in his senior year. Like Gregg DeSantis, who earned All-OVAC honors in football during his senior year at Weirton Madonna High School, Paul Vargo was All-OVAC Special Mention for basketball his senior year at Linsly. Not only was Jim Mellinger an All-County and All-Eastern Ohio selection in three sports, but he was also first-team All-OVAC in basketball and baseball and second-team All-OVAC in football. Steve Zaugg would later say he "...*never expected to make the team-the guys were so darn good.*"

In addition, over half of the players on the roster were housed in dorms (Bartell, Bonar, Krise, or Rogers Hall), with the majority assigned to Bonar Hall. Nearly two-thirds of the players had a car on campus.

Finally, for those bored with all the baseball stuff in this book and pining for something more celestial, the list of players includes one Capricorn (Price), one Aquarius (Duplaga), two Pisces (Bonar and Williams), two Aries (Stacy and Zaugg), two Taurus (Fabbro and Searage), two

Gemini (DeSantis and Frey), two Cancer (Dulkoski and Kertes), five Leo (DeMeo, Freshwater, Hynes, Mellinger, and West), four Libra (Lufft, Schmidt, Shepherd, and Spencer), two Scorpio (Anthony and Girty), and one Sagittarius (Vargo). There, I said it, so consider yourself included! You can thank me later.

With a headline of "Watson Sees Team 'With More Potential'" Shelly Romick writes in the October 2 edition of *The Trumpet*...

After coaching two consecutive West Virginia Intercollegiate Conference teams, Coach Jim Watson believes he may now have a baseball team with even more potential. A record 62 prospects are now participating in the fall baseball program which serves as six-weeks of try-outs, teaching clinic and intra-squad and varsity competition. As varsity competition, Watson fielded his players against the Warwood United Mineworkers League semi-pro team last Sunday for two, 7-inning games...The Hilltoppers host West Virginia University for another twin-bill at 1 p.m. Sunday, October 6, giving fans a preview of the '75 team. Only one player was lost to graduation from last year's talented squad - Steve Wojcik, a three-time All-Conference choice who was signed by the New York Mets organization...Returning lettermen, now going through fall drills, are David Williams, Robbie Schmidt, Jim Mellinger, Jon Kertes, Shawn Girty,...and Greg (sic) DeSantis. Williams, of Coshocton, Ohio, ranked eighth behind Wojcik, in the NAIA standings with a 1.10 ERA. After hurling a no-hitter against West Virginia Tech,

Williams finished the year with an 8-2 record and was listed as honorable mention on the All-Conference team along with Schmidt, at first base, and Mellinger in right. Kertes, power-hitting outfielder from Jewett, Ohio, and team captain, hit .418 to hold the highest batting average...Meanwhile, Mark Stacy, who was lost to the Hilltoppers last year due to mononucleosis, will be a strong possibility to move in at second. Girty, noted both for speed and defensive skill will again patrol the outfield with Kertes and Mellinger. Girty and DeSantis...were both selected honorable mention their rookie years to bring the total of West Liberty players chosen to 3 All-WVIAC and 5 honorable mention. Looking over candidates in daily workouts, Watson anticipates speed again to be a strong point. Incoming high school standouts include Rich Frye (sic), Baldwin High, Pittsburgh, Tom Lufft of Wheeling, who batted near .450 in American legion baseball, and Stan Duplaga, Linsly Institute, who could very possibly fill in the vacant third base position. Ray Searage, of Long Island, Mark Fabbro, Oak Glen High,... highlight the roster of 17 mound prospects which also includes sophomores Mike Anthony, Rick Bonar, and Ed Dulkoski...Last spring West Liberty clinched the Northern Division title of the WVIAC for the third straight year. They went on to sweep Morris Harvey to win the conference crown before bowing to Pembroke and Francis Marion as representatives of District 28 in the East Coast, Area 7, NAIA Tournament in Greenwood, South Carolina. The fall program

Dr. Michael F. Price

*enables Watson to evaluate prospects for next
spring and anticipate strengths and weaknesses.
Outstanding defense and speed will again be
characteristic of the team as viewed now. Aid
from the mound, however, could determine the
overall success of the spring campaign.
"The potential for this year's team is of the
highest quality," stated Watson after the first
week of fall training. "It largely depends on the
development of several young pitching prospects."*

Coach Watson would later tell Matt Mumley, Sports Editor of *The Trumpet*,

*If our younger pitchers come through to back up
veteran Dave Williams, and with our strong
defense and a blend of power and line-drive
hitters, we have an excellent chance of copping
the WVIAC crown for the third straight year.*

As fall ball came to a close and the equipment packed-up until informal practices resumed in January, several things had become apparent. First, nearly every player that had earned a place on the team had gained a certain degree of respect for his new teammates. The reverence was due to the skill that had been on display during the previous 6-weeks of try-outs. Equally important was that each player saw himself as a member of the team, a 24-member group, where each player had an important role. Above all, some friendships had been formed...friendships that would be forged from long van rides to away games. And as a result of these newly formed friendships, many of the players were given nicknames:

Rick DeMeo   Mouse, Mouseyboy
Mark Fabbro   Bear, Yogi

Gary Freshwater	Fresh
Rich Frey	Frenchy, Frenchman
Shawn Girty	Girt
Tommie Lufft	"T", Henry
Jim Mellinger	Melby
Mike Price	Piney, The Woodsman
Rick Spencer	Spence
Mark Stacy	Stace
Gary West	Harley
Steve Zaugg	Zaugger, Steveo

Left to right: Melby, Frenchy, Piney/The Woodsman

With the semester in full swing, things around campus had hit a frenetic pace. On Wednesday, October 2, the men's soccer team faced off against the Battlers of Alderson-Broaddus College, followed by games on Saturday with Wheeling College, and Tuesday against Point Park College. At the other end of campus, the Hilltop Players were preparing to raise the opening night curtain on their production of Emily Williams' *Night Must Fall*. Cast members include Sara Weidt, who plays an elderly aunt in the play. While many of the students may have been out the following night at the campus pub, it was not the case for the forty-or-so, second-year dental hygiene students who were receiving their caps. Here, the list includes Christie Derrow, Carol Goddard, and Janice Propchek. At about the same time, the members of Theta Xi were celebrating the completion of improvements to their fraternity house, including a new roof, additional showers, and a renovated recreation room, the Hilltopper football team was in Springfield, OH, facing a powerful Wittenberg College team. The Gold and Black would lose 27-3, dropping their overall record to 2-2.

Homecoming weekend activities kicked-off on Tuesday, October 8, with the movie *Let the Good Times Roll* showing in the Student Union, followed on Thursday with a performance by Cheech and Chong in the large gymnasium. With a demand for more cowbells at the football game on Saturday, the Theta Xi's set up a booth in the Student Union and began selling cowbells. The joint efforts of Phi Gamma Nu and Delta Sigma Pi proved successful as they were not only deemed the winner in the "best float" contest but also garnered the $75 first-place prize money. On the gridiron, the football team won a tough 29-22 win over West Virginia State. Capping off the special weekend was the crowning of Cathy DeFrances as Miss West Liberty 1974.

Needless to say, football was not the only sport happening on campus during the month. The soccer team continued its winning ways, while women's intramural tennis and men's intramural cross-country was underway. Speaking of intramurals, the October 16 edition of *The Trumpet* reports that Mark Stacy collected two-hits for his fraternity, Theta Xi, as they defeated the team from Delta Chi in a crucial matchup of softball powerhouses.

If nothing else, a student could make a trip down Route 88 to Wheeling to see a movie. Among the films was *The Taking of Pelham One Two Three*, starring Walter Matthau and Robert Shaw, *Texas Chainsaw Massacre*, or the recent premiere of *Airport 1975*, with Charlton Heston, George Kennedy, and Gloria Swanson.

Inning 3 (November 1974)

In baseball as in life,
all the important things happen at home.
(baseballrose.com)

In most ways, the month of November was much of the same for players and students since school began in August. Sure, the October mid-term exams were over, and the Thanksgiving break was just around the corner. Still, there was no coasting as things continued at a frantic pace.

Several of the players on the baseball team would eventually become members in a fraternity, including Mike Anthony (Chi Nu), Mark Fabbro and Jim Mellinger (Lambda Chi), and Gregg DeSantis, Gary Freshwater, Rich Frey, Ray Searage, Robbie Schmidt, Rick Spencer, and Mark Stacy (Theta Xi). In addition, the members of the team began selling raffle tickets to help finance the southern trip in March. Incidentally, the $100 first prize in the raffle was sold by Piney/The Woodsman to a former boss he had worked for in his hometown of New Martinsville. With the basketball season on the horizon, the members of the baseball team were asked to sign-up to sell refreshments during all home basketball games.

Above all, the time away from the baseball field allowed the players to concentrate on their studies. If a player did not obtain at

Lamdba pledges: Mark (Bear) Fabbro, top row, third from right

least an overall 1.6 GPA (grade point average) at the end of the fall semester, they would be ineligible to play baseball in the spring. Subsequently, most players would load-up on classes in the fall and take a much lighter load in the spring to better accommodate the spring baseball schedule.

At the same time, the players had to look ahead at what classes they would take in the spring since pre-registration for the coming semester was fast approaching (November 8). In planning their spring classes, players had to keep two things in mind.

First, players had to be enrolled in at least 12-hours of classroom work. This may sound like a light load, but considering the proposed thirty-four game spring schedule, along with nine of the games during the regular season away games, including three in the Charleston, West Virginia-area and two in the central part of the state, the 12-hour academic workload was far from light. Moreover, nine of the fifteen games between March 25, the first scheduled game of the regular season, and the last game of the regular season, scheduled for May 7, were weekday games. Besides, all but one…the game versus Marietta, which was a single, 9-inning game…were scheduled doubleheaders! Equally pressing, the players were advised to register for spring classes that were out as early as possible in the day since players were to be at the field between 10:00-10:30am on days when there was a home game to take batting practice.

Beyond the classwork, there were all the extracurricular things going on around campus, both good and not-so-good. On one side, not only was bus service between campus and Wheeling being discontinued and dogs no longer allowed in the Student Union, but the members of Theta Xi lost their (away) football game against the inmates being "lodged" at the state prison in nearby Moundsville, WV. The final score was 21-12, and the leading ground-gainer for the visitors was Gregg DeSantis with 100-rushing yards.

Conversely, tickets had gone on sale for the Seals and Croft concert at the Coliseum in Morgantown on November 23. The ticket prices ranged in price from $3.00-$5.00. Likewise, one might find enjoyment attending a lecture by the editor of the *Foxfire* series on Monday, November 11, in Wheeling, take in one of the final games of the season for the women's field hockey team, sign-up for intramural swimming, catch a women's volleyball game, or offer congratulations to the women's tennis team that finished 3rd in the WVIAC conference tournament. For those not into the sports scene and wanting to laugh a little, a double feature was showing in the Student Union on Saturday, November 9, starring the Marx Brothers in *Monkey Business* and *Horsefeathers*. Of course, there were always off-campus movies showing in Wheeling, including the recently released *The Life and Times of Grizzly Adams*. Throughout all the chaos, Robbie Schmidt still found time to win a turkey at the Theta Xi turkey shoot!

As students departed for the Thanksgiving break following the end of classes on Wednesday, November 27, their return to campus on Monday, December 2, meant one thing…final exams were less than two weeks away.

Inning 4 (December 1974)

People ask me what I do in winter
when there's no baseball. I'll tell you what I do.
I stare out the window and wait for spring.
(Rogers Hornsby)

As students resumed classes on the second day of December, they were met with temperatures in the low 30s and gusty winds out of the North. Worse, the temperatures did not rise above the 38-degree mark for the day. The cold temperatures were expected to continue through the end of the semester.

Within the gates of the school, Rick Bonar and Jon Kertes were named to the Dean's List for the fall semester. At the same time, Rick DeMeo was a member of the winning intramural swim team. In addition, the women's volleyball team ended the season with an 8-7 mark, the wrestling team was home on December 6 for their first home match of the year, and the men's basketball team kicked off the 74-75 season with home games against Beckley Junior College on December 7, followed by a WVIAC game against West Virginia Wesleyan the next night. The men's record currently stands at 1-3, and they will play two more games before the end of the year…at home against Ashland, OH, on December 11, and a road game against Middle Tennessee State College on December 14…to end the semester. The team will resume play on January 4. Don Jernigan placed 31st in the nation in the NAIA cross-country championships held in Salina, KS. His teammate, Bruce Cox, finished 154th in the national competition. Baseball pitcher Mark Fabbro finished second in the wrestling intramurals. Most impressive, the baseball players ended the fall semester with an approximate 2.6 GPA as a team.

Intramural Swim Champs: Mouseyboy front row, second from right

For others, two free concerts are coming up. The first one is on December 5 with performances by the Concert Band and Percussion Ensemble. The following night will be the Christmas Choral Concert. The final on-campus movie of the semester, *Massacre in Rome,* starring Richard Burton, will be showing at the Student Union on December 7. For those that desired to get off campus to see a movie, they had several choices. They could watch Steve McQueen, Faye Dunaway, and O.J. Simpson in *The Towering Inferno*; take in Mel Brooks' latest comedy, *Young Frankenstein*; catch Sean Connery as James Bond in *Man with the Golden Gun*; or Marlon Brando, Al Pacino, and a host of other big-name stars in the sequel, *Godfather II*.

As the last week of the semester commences, Dr. Ben Morton, Chancellor of the Board of Regents, has been chosen to address the nearly 235 seniors on December 15 as they receive their diploma. In addition to extra library hours, ARA (Aramark Food Services) announced they will be distributing free snacks from 9:00-10:00pm each night during exam week, December 16-20. And for those that may need a bit more than cookies and punch to get them through final exams, the college pub wants to remind students of the extended hours...Friday and Saturdays until 2:00am. For all the students who would rather stay in and watch tv between exams, December 20 not only signaled an end to the first half of the academic year but the ending of *The Newlywed Game* on ABC.

The college is closed for Christmas break beginning on December 21. The spring semester will officially start on Monday, January 13, with evening classes.

Dr. Michael F. Price

Inning 5 (January 1975)

Baseball statistics are like a girl in a bikini,
they show a lot, but not everything.
(Toby Harrah)

After a break of nearly three weeks, classes officially resumed meeting on Monday evening, January 13. The schedule of classes the first night of the spring semester included Business Statistics, Freshman (English) Composition, Foundations of Education, Foundations of Reading Instruction, Mathematics of Finance, Map Interpretation (Geography), Stage Band, and a basic concepts class in Political Science. As the evening classes began, the temperature was a chilly 22 degrees. When the classes were dismissed four hours later, the temperature had dropped six-degrees to an uncomfortable 16 degrees! The temperature for those that had early classes the next day was no different; however, the temperature at 8:00am on the first, full day of classes hovered around 13 degrees.

In most respects, the month of January was a solemn time for those that stayed around campus on the weekends. The scheduled Friday night movies for the month included *The Life and Times of Judge Roy Bean*, starring Paul Newman; *Mister Roberts* with Jack Lemmon and Henry Fonda; and *Serpico*, starring Al Pacino. On Saturdays, there was an opportunity to watch the undefeated wrestling team in the daytime, or the struggling men's basketball team at night. If nothing was going on, most students would slowly make their way to the cafeteria after sleeping until 12:00noon. After lunch, some would either go to the library and study or else sit in their dorm rooms and watch tv. This may explain why some students, including some on the baseball team, fell under-the-spell of the Freshman 15…gaining at least fifteen pounds during the winter months.

However, two events happened within days of each other that got everyone's attention. A case of food poisoning seems to have sent as many as sixty students to the infirmary seeking relief. However, the school's administration believed it may have been a combination of food poisoning and the seasonal flu. Equally newsworthy was the announcement from the school's athletics office that Tom Ackerman had tendered his resignation as the head coach of the men's basketball team.

The Tribune (Scranton, PA) in an article of January 24, shares that…

Tom Ackerman, in his sixth season as West Liberty's State's head basketball coach, has informed college officials he is resigning at the end of the season. Ackerman, whose current club has lost 14 of 17 games, indicated that he would like to remain in coaching but at the high school level. There was immediate speculation he would become a candidate for the head coaching position at the new Wheeling Park High School, which will consolidate Wheeling, Triadelphia, and Warwood high schools.
Ackerman coached Bethany College to a 24-12 record in two seasons before switching to West Liberty where his teams have won 62 and lost 89…

In a related story, *The Springfield News-Leader* (Springfield, MO.) of January 28 writes…

West Liberty State College athletic director Edgar Martin has announced that he will become the head coach of the Hilltoppers basketball team succeeding Tom Ackerman…

For the members of the baseball team that chose to stay around on the weekends, most weekends were busy, and the activities were commonly related to the upcoming season.

On Saturday mornings beginning at 9:00am, players were encouraged to go to the small gym and take batting practice. After both the netting of the batting cage and the pitching machine was set up, players would take turns either hitting or feeding baseball into the "jugs"…an electric pitching machine with two small wheels on top that sent baseballs hurling at the batter. After a few hours of hitting, the players would then make their way to the cafeteria for lunch in Rogers Hall. When the cafeteria closed, the players would return to their dorms until late afternoon when they would then make their way to outside the (large) gymnasium to begin selling refreshments at the men's basketball game that night. All proceeds from sales would offset the costs of the baseball team's southern trip in March. When Sunday afternoon arrived, most of the players would make their way to the library to study and prepare for the following week's classes.

Bowling Team: Frenchy, third from left; Mouseyboy, fourth from left

Throughout, Rick DeMeo and Rich Frey still had time to take their place on the school's bowling team, while Mike

Anthony was taking his place as runner-up in his weight class in intramural wrestling for his fraternity, Chi-Nu.

Intramural Wrestling Champs: Mike Anthony top row, first from left

Most exciting to the baseball players during January, however, was the sharing of the upcoming 34-game baseball schedule.

———————

The '75 schedule would kick-off with a 10-day southern trip to take place over the spring break. Here, the list of opponents included a single game with the University of North Carolina-Wilmington in Wilmington, NC, on Saturday, March 8; Jacksonville University in Jacksonville, FL, on Monday, March 10; Florida A & M University in Tallahassee, FL, on Wednesday, March 12; and Valdosta State University in Valdosta, GA, on Thursday, March 13. The final game of the southern trip will conclude with a match against Columbus College on Friday, March 14. All told, the southern schedule had the Hilltopper baseball team playing in three states, against five teams, and forty-five innings…in the course of a mere seven days!

Dr. Michael F. Price

Included in the twenty game conference schedule were games against traditional foes like Alderson-Broaddus, Concord, Davis and Elkins, Fairmont State, Morris Harvey, Glenville State, Salem, West Virginia State, West Virginia Tech, and the Bobcats of West Virginia Wesleyan. Of the conference games, West Liberty would host eight of the games...

Davis and Elkins	March 29
Salem	April 8
West Virginia Wesleyan	April 16
West Virginia Tech	May 3

The remainder of the games would have the Hilltoppers traveling in-state to conference games at...

Athens (Concord)	March 25
Charleston (Morris Harvey)	April 2
Glenville (Glenville State)	April 5
Institute (West Virginia State)	April 12
Fairmont (Fairmont State)	April 19
Philippi (Alderson-Broaddus)	April 22

Of the eight non-conference games, the schedule had West Liberty hosting in-state rival West Virginia University and Frostburg State (MD) for doubleheaders on April 11, and May 7. Additionally, the Hilltoppers had on their schedule non-conference, doubleheader, away games at California State College (PA) on April 21, and Steubenville College (OH) on April 26. Except for the games on the southern trip, which were a single, 9-inning game, and the single-game against Marietta College on March 27, the ten conference and four non-conference games were scheduled as doubleheaders to reduce travel expenses.

68

The Season That Was

1975 Schedule

Date	Opponent	Location
March 8	UNC-Wilmington	Wilmington, NC
March 10	Jacksonville U	Jacksonville, FL
March 12	Florida A&M	Tallahassee, FL
March 13	Valdosta State	Valdosta, GA
March 14	Columbus College	Columbus, GA
March 25*	Concord College	Athens, WV
March 27*	Marietta College	Marietta, OH
March 29*	Davis & Elkins Col.	West Liberty, WV
April 2*	Morris Harvey Col.	Charleston, WV
April 5*	Glenville State Col.	Glenville, WV
April 8*	Salem State Col.	West Liberty, WV
April 11	West Virginia Uni.	Morgantown, WV
April 12*	W Virginia State Col.	Institute, WV
April 16*	WV Wesleyan Col.	West Liberty, WV
April 19*	Fairmont State Col.	Fairmont, WV
April 21	California State Col.	California, PA
April 22*	Alderson-Broaddus Col.	Philippi, WV
April 26	Steubenville Col.	Steubenville, OH
May 3*	West Virginia Tech	West Liberty, WV
May 7	Frostburg State Col.	Frostburg, MD
May 10 - 11	WVIAC Conf. Tour.	Charleston, WV
May 19 - 23	Area 7	Playoffs TBD
May 30- June 4	NAIA College World Series	St. Joseph, MO

*denotes conference games

Most daunting could well be the caliber of the non-conference teams on the '75 schedule. The cumulative (1974) record for the ten teams (UNC-W, Jacksonville University, Florida A&M, Valdosta State College, Columbus College, Marietta College, West Virginia University, California State College, Steubenville College, and Frostburg College) was an unofficial 160 wins and 122 losses. The

1974 won-loss record of Florida A&M, Valdosta State College, and Marietta College combined stood at an intimidating 81 wins and 28 losses...a .743 winning percentage! On closer review, the 1974 records for several of the non-conference teams lined up this way...

UNC-W	participated in NAIA District 29 playoffs
Valdosta State	advanced to D-II college world series
Columbus Col.	participated in District 25 playoffs
Marietta Col.	between 1970-1974 was 113-33
Frostburg State	participated in District 18 playoffs

Placed side-by-side with the record of the Hilltopper teams of the past few years, the records of these non-conference teams had little to brag about. Since becoming head coach, Watson's three-year record (1972–1974) stands at an impressive 37 wins and 11 losses in conference games...a 78% winning percentage. During that same time, Coach Watson's teams won three Northern Division WVIAC titles (1972, 1973, 1974), two WVIAC titles (1973, 1974), were NAIA District 28 champs twice (1973, 1974), and represented District 28 in the Area 7 playoffs (1973, 1974).

Inning 6 (February 1975)

The other sports are just sports.
Baseball is a love.

In most ways, the month of February began with no shortage of on-campus happenings. Campus police report that both Krise Hall and Rogers Hall cafeterias were broken into sometime during the early morning hours of February 3. In addition to some vandalization, a reported $200-$400 was stolen. The first week or so also saw the men's intramural basketball begin with a flurry of games, the movie *Cool Hand Luke* with Paul Newman showing in the Student Union, and a new rule from the ARA that all students had to begin presenting their id's to get into the cafeterias. The weeks that followed saw no let-up with campus activities.

The Chi Nu fraternity was busy collecting funds to assist West Liberty's Ambulance Rescue Squad. Meanwhile, as Nancy Burgess was one of a group of co-eds pledging Chi Omega, and as Cathy Ford and Beth McVicker pledged Delta Zeta, several of the dental hygiene students from West Liberty were at the state prison in Moundsville cleaning the teeth of inmates, teaching dental hygiene, and educating them on proper dental care. As the Hilltopper bowling team continues its winning ways thanks in part to the efforts of Rich Frey and Rick DeMeo, Gary Freshwater and Robbie Schmidt are chosen as committee members of the Theta Xi pledge class, Ray Searage is being selected as a member of the men's intramural all-star basketball, and Jon Kertes was chosen captain of the '75 baseball team.

Jon Kertes

Dr. Michael F. Price

Upcoming movies at the Student Union include *Don't Look Now* with Julie Christie and Donald Sutherland, and *The Left Hand of God* starring Humphrey Bogart. Julian Bond, Georgia legislator, and the first African-American to be nominated for the vice-presidency, has been scheduled to speak at the Student Union on March 1.

Even though it was only February, most students had already begun looking toward March 7 and spring break. However, the baseball team's focus was more immediate...a full schedule of indoor practices.

Since the men's basketball program had priority over most everything pertaining to the big gym, and because there were usually afternoon classes being held in the small gym, the practice time and space for the baseball team was well organized.

On any given weekday practice, the baseball team divides into three groups, with each group going to one of three workout stations. While infielders were in the big gym taking ground balls, practicing double plays, etc., the pitchers were in the small gym throwing to catchers. Meanwhile, a third group, mostly outfielders, were in the lower hallway adjacent to the campus swimming pool, running sprints. After about a half-hour or so, the groups would change stations. The pitchers would go to lower hall and run sprints, the infielders would make their way into the small gym for batting practice, and the outfielders would go to the big gym. Around 30-minutes later, the groups would change stations a third, and final, time. The infielders would run sprints in the lower hallway of the building. The pitchers in the big gym would be hit ground balls and practice holding on runners, as the outfielders took batting practice. The two-hour sessions would commonly end with all the players meeting in the big gym to practice baserunning and simulate game situations since the team could not practice outside due to the cold weather.

Inning 7 (March 1975)

Baseball reveals character.
Golf exposes it.
(Ernie Banks)

Although forecasters predicted 3-5 inches of snow to blanket the area during the first few days of the month, the threat of bad weather did not adversely affect the events on or around campus. The March 3 blood drive was a big success with over 125 pints donated. It was recently announced that WLSC president, Dr. James Chapman, will visit China next month as part of a 21-member delegation of college and university presidents from across the U.S. Dr. Chapman will be the only college president from West Virginia to make the trip. Radio station WWVA in Wheeling is planning to air several "Music from the Campus" programs during the month, including a performance by the WLSC Concert Band and Stage Band on Tuesday, March 11, and one by the school's Concert Choir on Tuesday, March 25. In addition to finishing the regular season 19-1 and winning the WVIAC title by dethroning Fairmont State, nine of the team's wrestlers are off to participate in the NAIA national championships. As they leave, the team is ranked 9th in the country. While the women's basketball team ends the year with a 7-7 record, the men's season is also over thanks to a defeat by Shepherd College in the WVIAC tournament. Not only does the season come to an end for the men's team, but also the Hilltopper coaching career of head coach, Tom Ackerman, who announced his resignation in January. Planning is underway for Black Awareness Week scheduled for April 6-13 and Women's Week activities, April 7-10. Finally, the results of the campus-wide election survey showed that nearly half of the school's residents are in favor of either 24-hour visitation in single-sex halls or co-ed dorms. However, nothing is more anticipated than the start of the baseball season, which officially begins with the southern trip.

Bright and early on Friday, March 7, with temperatures in the upper 30's, a caravan of three vehicles, two 15-person school vans and Coach Watson driving his car, departed the West Liberty campus for the first southern trip in two years (the '74 trip was canceled because of gas shortages). Each van would carry half of the twenty-four players making the trip, their luggage, along with bats, batting helmets, and a variety of other items. At the time, the twenty-four players making the trip was the largest number to date. Also with the team were traveling secretary/statistician *par excellence*, Brent Long, and former Hilltopper pitcher, Steve Wojcik, a recent draft pick of the New York Mets, who was hitching a ride to Florida and the start of spring training in St. Petersburg. The older players would take turns as drivers.

Upon leaving the school, the route would take the team south on Route 88 toward Wheeling. There, the caravan will pick-up I-70 and travel west toward Cambridge, OH. Following a short, one-hour drive, the group will then turn due south on I-77. After driving nearly 300-miles through parts of West Virginia and Virginia, the caravan would meet up with I-40 on the perimeter of Winston-Salem, NC, and begin the last leg of the day's journey and the first opponent in the team's 5-game southern trip...the University of North Carolina-Wilmington.

Along the way, the stops were planned to be short ones to refuel the vans, change drivers, and to grab a "to go" meal from the small per diem (meal money) each player was given. All told, it was anticipated that the first leg of the '75 southern trip would take around 10-hours and cover nearly 650 miles.

As a public institution established in 1947 as a junior college, Wilmington College became a four-year college in 1963. When the school became part of the University of North Carolina system six-years later, it took on the University of North Carolina-Wilmington title. Located on the eastern end of the 2,500-mile long, I-40 corridor, Wilmington is not only the permanent home to the USS North Carolina but is also a popular beach destination. The school's student enrollment is around 3,000, slightly larger than West Liberty. It includes as one of its alumni, college basketball coach, John Calipari.

Many of the area newspapers were quick to pick-up on the team's southern trip by highlighting several players making the trip.

In the Monday, February 10, issue of the *Wheeling News-Register*, Nick Bedway notes that…

He's (Steve Wojcik) been working with West
Liberty Coach Jim Watson's hurlers during the
winter indoor conditioning program and shares
the youthful strategist's enthusiasm about the
current Hilltopper squad.

Sports Editor of the *Cambridge Daily Jeffersonian*, Steve Wyatt, writing in his column on March 12, shares the following…

Word received from West Liberty State College
in West Virginia, indicates that former Bobcat
Randy Shepherd may figure prominently in the
Hilltoppers' baseball plans this season. Shep, a
5'10", 180-pound junior, is currently, one of
the main catchers on the team. West Liberty,

and Shep, are currently in Florida for their
winter tour, then head to Georgia before
returning home. Love the sunshine.

On that same day, the *Weirton Daily Times* ran an article highlighting two of the local players, stating that …
Ex-Weirton Madonna diamond standout, Greg
(sic) DeSantis, who hails from Follansbee, is
listed as the starting catcher on West Liberty
State College's baseball team which opens the
season Saturday at the University of North
Carolina-Wilmington. DeSantis, returning
letterman, played second base last spring and
had a .312 batting average with 24 hits and 15
runs batted in. He is a sophomore. Gary
Freshwater, junior from Colliers, is listed on the
pitching staff.

An article appearing in the *Steubenville Herald-Star* of March 7 brought attention to another of the team's players, noting that…
(Dave) Williams had a 7-1 record on the mound
last year, allowing only 34 hits and 15 runs in
57 innings, while ranking fifth in the NAIA with
a 1.10 earned run average. The senior from
Coshocton, O, was drafted by the New York Mets
out of high school, and is sure to be the premiere
in the conference this spring.

Finally, an article in the *Wetzel Republican* (New Martinsville, WV) of March 13 reports that…
At West Liberty, New Martinsville is represented
by Michael Price, a 5'10", 160-pound outfielder.
Mike is a 20-year old history major and Spanish
minor, the son of Mary Lou Price. The Player

*Profile…says that he has good speed and is a fine
defensive outfielder and he is a transfer from
Miami Dade.*

Upon arriving in the late afternoon in Wilmington, the team was met with temperatures in the upper 60's…a much-welcomed feeling since the temperatures during early March in northern West Virginia commonly average in the mid-30s. The cold temperatures in the weeks leading up to the southern trip meant the team had no outdoor practices.

Arriving at the hotel in Wilmington, the unpacking was quick and easy since two players shared a suitcase to minimize space in the van. The equipment was guardedly left in the vans. From there, four players were assigned to each room with two players to a bed. Lights outs were 11:00pm. Before retiring, players were reminded that they must have eaten breakfast, dressed, and in the vans by mid-morning of the next day for the drive to the field and the 2:00pm game. Dave Williams is scheduled to pitch the opener for the Hilltoppers versus the Seahawks. In his 18th year as the head coach, Bill Brooks brings his team into the game with a 1-2 record, after splitting a doubleheader with NC State and losing to Duke. Brooks' record includes winning the National Junior college championship in 1961 and 1963.

As the first stop on the team's southern trip in 1973, the Hilltoppers divided a two-game series with the Seahawks, winning the first game 15-4 and losing the second one, 5-3.

Saturday, March 8 vs. UNC-W
(Overall record 0-0, Conference 0-0)
Beyond the United Nation's proclamation of the first International Women's Day and the weather conditions that included a temperature at game time in the high 50's and fair skies, there seems to be little written about the game beyond the following that appears in the Sunday, March 9, edition of

Dr. Michael F. Price

the *Wheeling News-Register* and entitled "W. Liberty Drops Opener in Twelfth" and reads…

> *The West Liberty State baseball team dropped its season opener here Saturday afternoon to the University of North Carolina-Wilmington, 4-3, in 12 innings. Coach Jim Watson's squad, which is on a five-game southern tour, played well in the opening outing as sophomore Greg (sic) DeSantis blasted a home run in the second inning and senior captain Jon Kertes smacked a round tripper in the fourth inning. Despite a lack of outdoor practice, the Hilltoppers did not have an error. After DeSantis' blast, Wilmington racked up three runs in the third off Dave Williams on two walks and two singles. West Liberty claimed another tally in the seventh when Jim Mellinger singles, moved to second on a wild pitch, and Tom Lufft, a freshman from Wheeling, singled him home. The winning run came when Wilmington's Mike Good singled, stole second and was driven in by Howie Edgerton's single with two outs. Bob Clements was the winning pitcher in relief, with six strikeouts and three walks, while Williams went the distance in the loss. Williams walked five and struck out five. The Hilltoppers had eight hits to six for the victors as DeSantis added a single to his home run and Stan Duplaga and Lufft had two singles each. West Liberty has today off and will meet the University of Jacksonville on Monday at 1 p.m.*

Of the game with the Seahawks, Sports Editor of *The Trumpet*, Matt Mumley, would add in a March 26 article, that…

The Season That Was

In their first outing the Hilltoppers played errorless ball.

As the teams walked off the field, the final tally reads...

West Liberty   3 runs   8 hits   0 errors
UNC-W   14 runs   6 hits   1 error
Williams (0-1) and DeSantis, Spencer (11)
Watkins, Clements (6) and Good.

With bags packed and vans loaded, the team headed west on I-40 just long enough to meet I-95. From there, the caravan turned south for a 6.5-hour, nearly 450-mile trip to the next stop on the southern tour...Jacksonville, Florida, and a Monday, March 10, 1:00pm scheduled game against the Jacksonville University Dolphins.

As with UNC-W, Jacksonville University is located not far from the easternmost point of a major interstate. In this case, it's I-10. Like UNC-W, Jacksonville University was established as a junior college (1934) and later granted status as a four-year college (1956). The school has a student enrollment of nearly 2,000. Among its list of alumni are NBA center, Artis Gilmore, and singer/actor, Terrance Mann. In his second year as the head coach of the Dolphin baseball team, Jack Lamabe, like Coach Watson, is a graduate of Springfield College in Massachusetts.

In the day leading up to the JU game, the team had the joy of touring the Montreal Expos' spring training facility in Daytona Beach, FL, along with taking in an exhibition game between the Expos and the Boston Red Sox. The game was made all the more meaningful when Brent Long presented Coach Watson, a lifelong Red Sox fan, with a ball autographed by Bosox pitcher Luis Tiant. Sadly, the Bosox lost 9-3. When Tiant was pulled in the fourth inning, the Red Sox were leading 2-1.

79

Dr. Michael F. Price

Monday, March 10 vs. Jacksonville University
(Overall record 0-1, Conference 0-0)
An article in the Tuesday, March 11, edition of the *Wheeling News-Register*, and entitled "Hilltoppers Downed By Dolphins," chronicles the game in the following manner...

The West Liberty State baseball team went
down to its second loss in two outings on its
southern tour as Jacksonville University tallied
two runs in the fifth inning and five in the
seventh to beat the Hilltoppers 9-3. West Liberty
was leading 3-2 in the fifth inning behind pitcher
Ray Searage before Robin Roberts Jr., son of the
former Phillies pitching star, knocked in two
runs with a single. Don Wallace delivered a
three-run double for the Dolphins to highlight
the five-run seventh inning. Searage, though
yielding a just one earned run, was tagged with
the loss while Lenny Locasscio went six innings
in picking up the win for the Dolphins, who
were playing in their 15ᵗʰ game of the season.
The temperature at game time Monday in
Jacksonville was 80 degrees.

Matt Mumley, Sports Editor of the WLSC newspaper, *The Trumpet*, noted in an article dated March 26 that Hilltopper pitcher, Ray Searage, was impressive despite being shackled with the loss...

Freshman Ray Searage was the losing pitcher,
going 6 2/3 innings with five hits and six whiffs.

Mumley would go on to write in the same article that...
...Kertes had a two run double while Jim
Mellinger, Duplaga, and DeSantis each smacked
a double.

West Liberty   3 runs   7 hits   6 errors
Jacksonville Univ   9 runs   7 hits   3 errors
  Searage (LP 0-1, SO 6, W 4), Fabbro (7), (SO 1, W 0)
  DeSantis, Duplaga D; Kertes D, 2 RBI's; Mellinger D, S,
  RBI
  Locasscio (WP), Kluber (7), and Winn, Searangella 2S;
  Roberts, Jr, S, 2 RBI's; Wallace D, 3 RBI's

Jacksonville University would go on to finish the season 21-35, a marginal improvement over the 1974 record, which saw the team finish at 18-37. Next up for the Hilltoppers was a date with the NCAA Division I Rattlers of Florida A&M, a member of the Mid-Eastern Athletic Conference, and their head coach, Costa "Pop" Kittles, who has been at the helm of the Rattlers' baseball program for fifteen years.

Considering the team had traveled nearly 1,100 miles since leaving the West Liberty campus, traveled through no less than six states, and played nineteen innings of baseball over the course of five days, the three-hour, 175-mile drive west on I-10 from Jacksonville to Tallahassee seemed to most players a short one. The Hilltoppers would need all the energy they could muster because A&M was not only riding a seven-game winning streak but also had one of the best players in the country in Andre Dawson.

Established in 1887 as part of the second Morrill Land Grant Act, Florida Agriculture and Mechanical...FL A&M for short...is one of the largest schools associated with the HBCU (Historically Black Colleges and Universities) design. With nearly 4,000 students, the school is the only HBCU in the state of Florida. The list of alumni includes Althea Gibson (tennis great and former pro golfer), Olympic sprinter Bob Hayes, sports announcer Pam Oliver, Meadowlark

Lemon, and actor Meshach Taylor (CBS sitcom Designing Women),

Wednesday, March 12, vs. Florida A&M University
(Overall record 0-2, Conference 0-0)
With temperatures in the high 70's and winds gusting at times to 25mph, the Hilltoppers won the game 6-2 behind strong pitching and clutch hitting.

An article appearing in the *Tallahassee Democrat*, the day after the game, summed up the game by saying...
The Hilltoppers of West Liberty State (W.Va.)
ended Florida A&M's unbeaten baseball string
Wednesday afternoon, by stopping the Rattlers
6-2 on the A&M field. Gary Freshwater
picked up his first victory of the season,
limiting the Rattlers, now 7-1, to five hits and
one run before yielding to Daryll Costa (sic) in
the eighth. The win was also the first of the
season for the Hilltoppers, now 1-2. The
Rattlers were able to get only one single a piece
from Joseph Hicks, Andre Dawson, Waymon
Winton, Gene Harris, and Joe Durante.
Ephraim Riggins, 1-1, suffered the loss. He
allowed eight hits and three runs in seven
innings. Joseph Tolliver came on in relief and
was tagged for the other three runs on five hits.
Jon Kertes went four-for-five, including a
booming triple, and drive in three runs. Stan
Duplhea (sic) added two doubles and a rbi for
the Hilltoppers. West Liberty State jumped out
in front in the first with a pair of runs behind
three hits, one of them a double by Duplhea (sic),
and a rbi single by Kertes. A&M came back in
the bottom of the inning to slice the lead in half
when second baseman William Campbell walked

and later scored on a sacrifice fly by catcher
James Brockenbury. West Liberty scored the
winning run in the seventh on Gary West's
sacrifice fly that drove in Tom Luffe (sic). A&M
added its other run in the bottom of the eighth
when the Rattlers had the bases loaded with none
out and Hicks scored on Winton's double play
grounder.

In an article entitled "W. Liberty Chalks Up First Nod," the *Wheeling News-Register* summed up the game by saying…

…Breaking a two-game losing streak, the
Hilltoppers rode the strong seven-inning pitching
of Gary Freshwater and two innings of steady
relief work by Ed Dulkoski to upend Florida A&M
by a 6-2 score yesterday in Tallahassee. The
defeat ended the seven-game winning streak of the
hosts. Freshwater struck out six and walked four
during his stint on the mound, combining with
Dulkoski to limit the hosts to just five hits.
Meanwhile, West Liberty was collecting 12 hits
off a pair of Florida A&M hurlers. Senior
outfielder Jon Kertes paced the batting
assault for the winners, drilling a triple while
knocking in three runs. With two hits each
were Greg (sic) DeSantis, Stan Duplaga, who
rapped a pair of doubles, and Robbie Schmidt,
while Jim Mellinger singled across a run.
Mellinger and Duplaga had run scoring hits in
the first inning, while West Liberty wrapped up
the game with two more tallies in the ninth,
both of which were knocked in by Kertes'
triple.

West Liberty   6 runs   13 hits   1 error
Florida A&M   2 runs   5 hits   2 errors
   Freshwater (WP), Dulkoski (8), and DeSantis
   Riggins (LP), Oliver (8) and Brock

In the March 26 issue of the Hilltopper school newspaper, *The Trumpet*, Sports Editor, Matt Mumley, would add to the game results by writing...
   ...Gary Freshwater was the winning pitcher
   with relief from Ed Dulkoski. Duplaga had two
   doubles, while DeSantis, Kertes, and Robbie
   Schmidt had two singles each and Shawn Girty,
   Mark Stacy, and Jim Mellinger each had a
   bingle.

Although the box scores for this particular game were unavailable, the Rattlers would win seventeen of their next twenty-two games and end the year with an impressive 24-6 mark. Andre Dawson would leave A&M after the academic year was complete and would end up being drafted that year by the Montreal Expos in the eighth round. The Hilltoppers came away from the A&M game having learned a valuable lesson: namely, never, never, wear the uniform with the player's name on the back of the jersey to an away game! Need I say more.

With 60% of the games of the southern trip behind them, and sporting an overall record of 1-2, the team prepared for the short 90-minute, 75-mile drive north and the next day's opponent...Valdosta State College.

Located within the city of Valdosta, approximately 20-minutes north of the Georgia-Florida border, Valdosta State College was founded as a public institution in 1906, but did not open until 1913 for financial reasons, and then, as an all-female school for teachers. Nearly four decades later, in

1950, the school became co-ed. Student enrollment is over 4,200. In an ESPN, nationwide poll, the city of Valdosta was voted TitleTown because of all the district, regional and national titles won by the school in baseball, football, tennis, and in women's softball...three national champion-ships...two in football and one in men's tennis...between 2000-2010. Alumni of the school include Nancy Grace, TV personality; Lisa Blount, the award-winning actress who played Lynette Pomeroy in *An Officer and a Gentleman*; Pauley Perrette, regular on *NCIS*; Jessie Tuggle, linebacker, Atlanta Falcons; and numerous college football coaches, including Dana Holgorsen, Mike Leach, Will Muschamp, and Kirby Smart. In his 8th year as head of the VSC baseball program is coach Tommy Thomas. Beyond returning 10 lettermen and a 38-13 record in '74, the team was also coming off a trip to the NCAA Division II College World Series.

Thursday, March 13 vs. Valdosta State College
(Overall record 1-2, Conference 0-0)

Other than the Hilltoppers losing another one-run, extra-inning game, this time, an 11-innings by a score of 3-2, and that the Hilltoppers faced one of Valdosta's best pitchers, second-team All-American, Steve McDiffitt, little was found about the game that was played with temperatures in the mid-80s with wind gusts reaching 30mph.

Sports Editor of *The Trumpet*, Matt Mumley, in an article that appears in the campus newspaper on March 23, writes that in the game against VSC...

Kertes and Stacy had two singles each while
Girty had a base hit. Williams went 10 innings
with Rick Bonar going the last inning and
picking up the loss.

Dr. Michael F. Price

"Ex-Magnolia Star Stops W. Liberty" reads the headline in the March 14 edition of the *Wheeling News-Register.*

...the Hilltoppers record dipped to 1-3 yesterday as they sustained a 3-2 setback in 11 innings at Valdosta (Ga.) State campus. It was the second extra-inning loss on the trip for Coach Jim Watson's club, which is slated to spend Saturday on holiday in Atlanta before heading home. Getting the pitching win for Valdosta was ex-Magnolia High righthander Steve McDiffitt, who went the distance and gave up only five hits. A sophomore, McDiffitt struck out eight and walked five. He surrendered two runs in the fourth inning after the first West Liberty batter reached base on an error. A walk, singles by Jon Kertes and Mark Stacy and Stan Duplaga's sacrifice fly plated the runs. Dave Williams, who pitched all 12 innings in losing to North Carolina-Wilmington in the opener last Saturday, worked ten frames yesterday and blanked the Georgia squad after giving up a pair of runs in the first inning. Williams was lifted in the 11th and the loss went to Rick Bonar, who walked lead off batter Jeff Greenlaigh, who later came around on a sacrifice bunt, an infield error, and a wild pitch. Kertes and Stacy got two hits each off McDiffitt to pace the West Liberty attack...

Quoting Coach Watson and the teams' play so far during the southern trip, Mumley goes on to write...

We played extremely well considering we didn't have a practice outside before we left. However, our clutch hitting didn't come through but that takes time. Our pitching was excellent

(2.19 ERA in four games), and every one of our pitchers had a chance. They made some mental mistakes but those can be corrected.

In passing, the VSC starting pitcher that day, Steve McDiffitt, and Piney/the Woodsman were from the same town, New Martinsville, WV, and played baseball together all through high school. In the later innings of the game, Piney was sent into first base to pinch run. After seeing who it was that had come in, McDiffitt's first throw was not to the catcher but to first base. Naturally, a smile came on both player's faces! In fact, the story has it that McDiffitt would throw over to first several more times before he would get the last out of the inning.

The Blazers would go on to win 2-out-of-every-3 games and finish the year with an impressive 36-18 record. McDiffitt, along with several of his teammates from the '75 team, would later be drafted into the pros.

With vans loaded, the Hilltoppers, now a respectable 1-3, began making the three-hour, 175-mile drive north for a fifth and final game on the southern tour with the Cougars of Columbus College.

Established in 1958 as a public, junior college, Columbus College was granted status as a four-year institution in 1965. The student enrollment is just over 3,600. Located approximately 100-miles south and west of Atlanta, the city of Columbus lies on the east bank of the Chattahoochee River, and across the river from Phenix City, Alabama. As expected, the college takes its name after the city that surrounds it. Cougar alumni include Joni Ernst, junior U.S. senator from Iowa, and Jim "Bones" Mackay, who caddied for Phil Mickelson for nearly a quarter of a century. Charles Ragsdale begins his 6th season as head coach. His team comes off a '74 showing in the District 28 playoffs and a respectable overall record of 27-24.

Friday, March 14 vs. Columbus College
(Overall record 1-3, Conference 0-0)

Early that morning, Coach Watson notified the players that the 12:00noon game was being canceled due to rain the previous day. Columbus College would participate in the 1975 South Atlantic Region, NCAA Division II playoffs, a region that included eventual College World Series winner Florida Southern. The CC Cougars would end the '75 season with a record of 32-19 and a .627 winning percentage. While the rain-out brought an "official" end to the scheduled games of the southern trip, one can only imagine what might have been, especially considering the surging Hilltoppers were scoring an average of nearly 5 runs a game and allowing only 2 per nine innings in their previous four games.

With the game canceled, the team loaded the vans in preparation for the final leg of the trip home. But before beginning the nearly 800-mile, 12-hour journey back to West Liberty, the group would spend the day, Saturday, March 16, taking in the sites of Underground Atlanta, along with an NBA game between the Atlanta Hawks and the Philadelphia' 76ers, which were led by all-star Darrell Dawkins.

The next day, the 3-vehicle caravan left Atlanta. This time, the route would take the team through northern Georgia, Tennessee, Kentucky, and Ohio. Outside of Cincinnati, the caravan would jump on I-71 toward Columbus. From there, the team would head due east on I-70 toward Wheeling, and then Route 88 north toward the West Liberty campus.

With the southern trip in the rearview mirror, the team arrived back in West Liberty safe-and-sound not long before spring classes resumed on Monday, March 17. Sadly, the players were met with temperatures that were nearly forty-degrees lower from what they had experienced in Georgia some 36-hours prior. Still, the rained-out game with Columbus College on Friday, March 14, proved to be a welcome break considering all that had taken place between Friday, March 7, and Sunday, March 16.

In general terms, the team had been in no less than five states (Virginia, North Carolina, South Carolina, Georgia, and Florida) since leaving West Virginia, traveled over 2,100 miles, stayed in no fewer than seven different hotels, played a total of thirty-seven innings of baseball, and all of this in the course of a mere 10-days! However, more impressive was the sheer grit and caliber of play displayed by Coach Watson's players during that four-game schedule. While the team ended up with a respectable 1-3 record, two of the three losses were by one run. More, each of the opponents played during the southern trip could boast of their own accolades.

The Seahawks of UNC-W will win twenty-six more games, win the District 29 playoffs, and play in the 1975 NAIA World Series in St. Joseph, MO. Despite ending the year with a 21-35 record, Jacksonville University had one of its players, a pitcher, taken in the seventh round of the 1975 baseball draft by the Milwaukee Brewers. Considering that Florida A&M would end-up losing only five more games all season and winning twenty-five in total, the Hilltopper 6-2 win against the Rattlers was all the more impressive because of one of its most heralded players, Andre Dawson.

In 1974, the future 8-time National League All-Star, Rookie of the Year (1977), and National League MVP (1987), ranked 3rd in the NCAA D-II with eleven doubles in twenty-seven games. His slugging percentage of nearly .700 placed him among the top 10 in the nation among all NCAA D-II schools. The previous year also saw Dawson lead his team in games played, at-bats, runs scored, hits, doubles, HR's, and rbi's. At Valdosta, the Hilltoppers would not only face one of the best pitchers in the NCAA D-II, but a team coming off an appearance in the 1974 NCAA Division II College World Series and loaded with several players that would later find themselves on the list of VSC all-time greats. The Cougars of Columbus College would finish the season 32-19 and participate in the regional playoffs.

In all, the four teams the 'Toppers faced during the southern trip (the University of North Carolina-Wilmington, Jacksonville University, Florida A&M, and Valdosta State) would end the '75 season with a combined 109 wins against 69 losses. And if one were to add the final record of Columbus College to those numbers, the figures would jump to an impressive 140 wins and 88 losses! Above all, the 1-3 record for the Hilltoppers was manageable since four of the five opponents on the schedule had a larger student body than WLSC...only Jacksonville University was smaller.

In the March 26 issue of *The Trumpet*, Sports Editor, Matt Mumley, would comment, saying...

*Coach Watson's team looked impressive in
their annual Southern trip even though the
'Toppers won only one contest.*

Although the daily temperatures hovered in the upper 40's or low 50's the week following the team's return from the southern trip, the Hilltoppers still managed several outside practices, something the team was unable to do before their journey south. The workouts were crucial as the team prepared to begin its conference schedule on Tuesday, March 25, against the Mountain Lions of Concord College, followed by the home opener against Davis and Elkins College, four days later on Saturday, March 29. In between, the Hilltoppers would play a single-game against perennial powerhouse Marietta College on their field on Thursday, March 27.

In anticipation of the doubleheader with Concord and the single-game against Marietta, the *Steubenville Herald-Star*, of Monday, March 24, records that…

> *Coach Watson expects to start Dave Williams*
> *and Gary Freshwater on the mound against*
> *the Mountain Lions and will probably send*
> *southpaw Ray Searage against Marietta.*

———————

Located in extreme southern West Virginia and less than a thirty-minute drive from the Virginia border, Concord College was founded in 1872 by veterans of the Union and the Confederacy. The school has an enrollment of just over 1,600 students and counts among its alumni, Freida Riley, the teacher made famous in the 1999 movie, *October Sky*. Since the Concord trip would involve one of the longest the Hilltoppers would take for a conference game, the team left on Monday, March 24, for the nearly 300-mile, approximate 5-hour trip. Moreover, the vans carried twenty-three players to Athens because one of the guys on the roster was left behind to address academic issues. The three-vehicle caravan arrived late afternoon and settled into their rooms. Concord is coached by Chuck Lambert.

Tuesday, March 25 vs. Concord College
(Overall record 1-3, Conference 0-0)

Writing in an article that appeared in the March 28 edition of the *Bluefield Daily Telegraph*, sportswriter Stubby Currence, notes that…

> *Concord baseball coach Chuck Lambert has seven*
> *returning letter winners on this year's roster.*
> *Lettermen include pitcher Ronnie Parker,*
> *catchers Tony Gometz and Jerry Epperly and*
> *infielders Jerry Groves, Alex Zachwieja, and*
> *Bill Compton. Lambert indicated that his*
> *starting pitchers for today's games will be*

*Parker and Randy Taylor. Top relief pitchers
will be Jerry Dresel and Sam Spencer. The
Concord lineups for the two games Gometz,
Epperly, or Al Bertwell behind the plate, either
Compton of Chuck Brooks at first base, either
Alex Zachwieja, Chuck Shaw or Bertwell at
second, either Jerry Groves or Jeff Bailey at
third, or either Gary Huff or Mark Blevins at
shortstop. Leading outfield candidates for
Concord are Alex Castaneda, Jerry
McClintic, James Tunstalle, Robert
Boroski, and Don Fouracre. Today's season
opener for Concord will mark the first of ten
scheduled doubleheaders this season for
Lambert's Lions.*

The game was rained out...good thing. With mostly
cloudy skies and wind gusts reaching 29mph, the game-time
temperature was a breezy 49 degrees. The temperature at
5:00pm was a chilling 37 degrees. The Mountain Lions
would end their season 8-8.

Following a day to recover from the long road trip to
Concord, the team headed back out on the road for a single-
game with a non-conference opponent...the Marietta
Pioneers.

By most standards, the one way, one-hour, forty-five
minute, 100-mile drive from West Liberty to Marietta would
take the team along a familiar route. First south on Route 88,
then I-70 west toward Cambridge, OH, and then south on I-
77 for less than one hour. Named in honor of French Queen
Marie Antoinette, the city of Marietta can boast as the first
permanent settlement in the Northwest Territory. Less than
four decades after the town's founding, Marietta College was
established in 1835, a scant two years before the beginning

of West Liberty. Located in the heart of the city, the private, liberal arts school boasts a student enrollment of around 1,800. In the years surrounding the American Civil War, it is widely believed that both the city of Marietta and the college was a "stop" along the famous Underground Railroad, a system of covert routes and safe houses for those escaping slavery in nearby Virginia and beyond.

Just as historic but more imposing is the baseball program at the college. The team is coached by Don Schaly, who is in his 12th year at the helm of the Pioneers. During the previous 5-years (1970-1974), the team has amassed 113 wins against a meager 39 losses. In 1974 alone, the team ended the year with a 22-12 record. The game between West Liberty and Marietta College would continue a rivalry dating back to 1964.

Thursday, March 27 vs. Marietta College
(Overall record 1-3, Conference 0-0)

The Pioneers come into the game sporting an 8-2 record with losses at the hands of Auburn and Georgia Tech. Sadly, the Hilltoppers would lose yet another one-run game, this time 4-3. The defeat would mark the third time in the young season that the Hilltoppers would lose a one-run game (UNC-W 4-3, and Valdosta 3-2).

In an article with the byline "Hilltoppers Play Pair At Concord," the piece shares…

The Gold and Black began the Northern
portion of its schedule yesterday afternoon in
losing a 4-3 heart-breaker, dropping the overall
record. Three of the defeats and the one victory
came during the annual spring junket earlier
this month. Saddled with the pitching defeat
was freshman righthander Mark Fabbro, who
turned in a sharp performance by yielding only
two hits and a pair of walks but was let down by

Dr. Michael F. Price

*his own defense which was charged with three
errors. West Liberty out-hit the hosts by 7-2,
but all of the safeties in the contest were singles.
Jim Mellinger, Mark Stacy, and Gary West had
RBI hits for the Hilltoppers. Marietta raised its
record to 10-2 in the contest, scoring what
proved to be the winning tally in the bottom of
the sixth inning. Handling the catching duties
for the Pioneers was former Bellaire St. John's
Central baseball star Joe Yazombek.* *

An article entitled "WLS Loses to Marietta," reported on
the one-run loss by saying...

*West Liberty State's baseball team squandered
an excellent pitching outing by Oak Glen High
product Mark Fabbro Thursday afternoon as the
Hilltoppers fell to host Marietta College, 4-3.
Fabbro, a freshman, allowed just one earned
run and two hits in his route-going performance
but the 'Toppers committed three errors, all of
which proved crucial. Absorbing their third
one-run loss of the year as their record dipped
to 1-4, the 'Toppers allowed the winning run to
score in the bottom of the sixth on a sacrifice
fly after errors on catcher Greg (sic) DeSantis
and third baseman Stan Duplaga had put two
Pioneer runners on base with none out.
Marietta jumped to a 3-0 lead before West
Liberty tied the game with single runs in the
fourth, fifth, and sixth frames. The win was the
tenth for the host Pioneers in 12 starts...* *

| West Liberty | 3 runs | 7 hits | 3 errors |
| Marietta | 4 runs | 5 hits | 2 errors |

The Season That Was

WLS- Fabbro, LP, (SO1 W2) and DeSantis; seven singles; Mellinger S, RBI, Stacy S, RBI, West, S, RBI M-Robinson, WP, (SO3, W1), Settles (6) (SO4, W2), and Yazombek, Bauer S, RBI, Leveck S.

The Pioneers would end the season with an overall record of 44-6, 16-0 in the Ohio Valley Conference, and runner-up in the 1975 NCAA, Division II, World Series. While the coach, Don Schaly, would be named the Coach of the Year, Marietta catcher, Joe Yazombek, would be selected as the series most valuable player.

With the first full month of games in *The Season That Was* in the books, the Hilltoppers' overall record stands at 1-4 and 0-0 in conference games. Except for three non-conference games in the coming month against West Virginia University, California St. (PA), and Steubenville College (OH), the team could now turn its attention to the fourteen conference games. By the end of April, the schedule will have had the team play in twenty games, some 140-innings, and travel over 1,600 miles. The month would kick-off with a doubleheader, make-up game against Davis and Elkins, followed by a twin bill against conference foe, the Golden Eagles of Morris Harvey College, on April 2.

Dr. Michael F. Price

Inning 8 (April 1975)

Baseball games are like snowflakes and
fingerprints, no two are ever alike.
(W.P. Kinsella)

Beyond being located about 2-hours east of the state capital of Charleston, Davis and Elkins College is an alcohol-free, private college related to the Presbyterian Church (USA). It is the smallest of the ten schools in the conference with just under 800 students. Founded in 1904, it stands as the "youngest" of the current 10-member WVIAC. Among the list of alums of the school is Petar (sic) "Press" Maravich, who coached D&E's basketball team for several years in the 1950s, and the father of LSU and NBA great, "Pistol Pete" Maravich. Beginning his third year as the Senator's head coach is David Barb, who's 1974 team finished 10-16.

The game was initially scheduled to be played on Saturday, March 29. However, an article that appears in *Wheeling News-Register* on Monday, March 31, entitled "Hilltoppers Idled Again," relates why the game was not played on that date.

Forced to call off the doubleheader for the
third time in four days, West Liberty State
College baseball team hopes to launch its West
Virginia Intercollegiate Conference title defense
on the host field tomorrow at 1 p.m. against
Davis and Elkins. The twinbill was originally
slated for Saturday but was wiped out because
of rain and reset for today. However, cold
weather and wet grounds again forced another
postponement.

Tuesday, April 1 vs. Davis & Elkins College
(Overall record 1-4, Conference 0-0)

Despite the sunny skies, the 50-degree temperature at the start of the first game of the doubleheader, and winds from the northwest gusting to 25mph, the temperature on the field felt as if it was in the lower 40's. As the final out was made at the second game, the temperature had shot-up to a poultry 51 degrees!

With the article entitled "WLS Gains Loop Sweep," the games were summed up this way…

West Liberty State opened the West Virginia Conference portion of its baseball schedule Tuesday afternoon at home under sunny skies by dumping Davis and Elkins (0-4) in a twinbill by 5-3 and 7-2. Though outhit 7-6 in the opener, the Hilltoppers got a strong mound effort from Ray Searage, who blanked the Senators until the sixth when the visitors erupted for three runs. Searage then got relief help from Oak Glen freshman Mark Fabbro to stem the tide. The 'Toppers then piled up a 5-1 lead in the second game behind a nine-hit batting attack and a route-going mound performance by River High's Rick Bonar for the 7-2 triumph. Freshman catcher Greg (sic) DeSantis from Weirton Madonna had two singles while Gary West had a two-run double in the front game. Robbie Schmidt then blasted a homer and two singles while West had another two-run double; Rick Spencer had a two-run triple; and Shawn Girty had three singles in the second game. WLS, now 3-4 overall, faces a key league twinbill Wednesday at perennial league power Morris Harvey. *

"*Hilltoppers Win 2, Face Morris Harvey*" was the lead in the April 2 edition of the *Wheeling News-Register*, and the writer saw things this way...

...Fine pitching from right-hander (sic) Ray Searage and a game saving relief effort by Mark Fabbro keyed a 5-3 triumph in the opener, while Rick Bonar tossed a four-hitter and Robbie Schmidt broke out of his batting slump with three hits in a 7-2 nightcap nod. The twin wins raised West Liberty's overall record to 3-4 , but Jim Watson's hustling squad is 2-0 against WVIC opposition as it shoots for a fourth straight Northern Division crown. Back -to-back doubles by Stan Duplaga and designated hitter Gary West gave Searage a 1-0 lead in the second inning of yesterday's opener. The Hilltoppers then took advantage of wildness by Senators starter Rick Jenkins to tally four runs in the bottom of the fifth. Three walks, a hit batsman, West sacrifice squeeze bunt and an infield out led to the runs. Searage, making his second pitching appearance since the southern trip in early March, tired in the sixth frame when he served a two-run homer to Jim Allen and a solo shot to Bruce Fleshman. In the seventh Searage was relieved with two on and one out by Fabbro, who closed the game with an infield out and by spearing a hot liner through the box that was ticketed for base hit territory. Bonar struck out six and walked four in the second game and he was in complete command after a four-run Hilltopper outburst in the fifth inning broke a 1-1 tie. Schmidt, who was two or 18

*entering the twinbill and went hitless in the
opener, snapped out of it with a home run and
a pair of singles. Leadoff batter Shawn Girty
collected three hits for a total of four for the
day, while Rick Spencer clouted a two-run triple.
West also contributed again as the DH, belting
a two-run double for a total of four RBI's.*

The April 11 issue of *The Trumpet* begins by noting that
the Hilltoppers conference record now stands at 4-0 and 5-4
overall (sic) following a doubleheader victory over Davis and
Elkins.

*In the front game of the Davis and Elkins
contest, Freshman Ray Searage pitched the
'Toppers to a 5-3 win, as Gary West belted a
two-run double and Gregg DeSantis rapped two
singles. Stan Duplaga had a double, while Tom
Lufft and Shawn Girty each had singles. In the
nightcap, WL scored a 7-2 victory as Robbie
Schmidt blasted a home run and two singles and
Rick Spencer tripled. Girty had two singles,
while Mark Stacy, DeSantis, Jon Kertes, and
Rich Frey each had a single. Rick Bonar was
the winning pitcher.*

West Liberty 5 D&E 3
(First Game)

Davis & Elkins	3 runs	7 hits	1 error
West Liberty	5 runs	6 hits	1 error

WL-Searage, wp (SO W3), Fabbro (7) and DeSantis;
DeSantis 2S, West D, 2rbi's
DE-Jenkins, 1p (SO5, W5), Crozier (5) and Collett; Allen
HR, S; Fleshman HR

Dr. Michael F. Price

West Liberty 7 D&E 2
(Second Game)

| *West Liberty* | *7 runs* | *9 hits* | *1 error* |
| *Davis & Elkins* | *2 runs* | *4 hits* | *3 errors* |

WL-Bonar, wp (SO6 W4) and DeSantis; Girty 3S; West D, 2rbi's; Spencer T, 2rbi's; Schmidt HR, 2S
LP-Allen, 1p (SO3 W3) and Collett, Mattice HR, S

The Senators would end the season 8-16 overall.

Located initially in Barboursville, West Virginia, a city several miles to the east of Huntington, Morris Harvey College is a private school established in 1888 by the Methodist Episcopal Church South. In the mid-1930s, the school moved to the city of Charleston. The college would make its final move to the current location in the late 1940s. Named after the owner of a coal mine who pitched-in during the early years of the 20th century to assist the school in overcoming its financial struggles, Morris Harvey College has an enrollment of just over 1,600 students. The school counts as one of its more noted alumni, former college basketball coach, Jim Harrick. The baseball team is coached by Tom Nozica, who has been at the helm of the team since 1969.

Wednesday, April 2 vs. Morris Harvey College
(Overall record 3-4, Conference 2-0)

The temperature at first pitch...1:00pm...was a comfortable 72 degrees. This was quite a change since the temperature at 8:00am was just above freezing! By the end of the second game, the temperature had risen to a comfortable 75 degrees. In addition to fair skies and a light wind, the conditions were perfect for baseball, so the teams followed the advice of Chicago Cubs great, Ernie Banks, and played two.

"Williams, Freshwater Sparkle in WLS Sweep," were the headlines, while the article went on to say…

Senior Dave Williams and Junior Gary Freshwater turned in a pair of shutout pitching performances Wednesday afternoon was West Liberty State won a key early-season West Virginia Conference doubleheader over host Morris Harvey at Watt Powell Park. Winning its second WVC twinbill in as many days, WL got a one-hit effort from Williams in the front game in an 8-0 win and Freshwater then mastered the Golden Eagles by 2-0 in the night cap. Williams, the Coshocton, O, senior, was nothing short of sensational. The only hit he allowed was a game-opening double by Gerald Givens, a looping drive just over the shortstop Tom Lufft's head, before the righthander mowed down 10 straight batters. Following a WLS error, Williams retired 12 more batters in succession before giving up his only walk of the day. Williams, a former New York Mets' draftee, fanned nine batters and got plenty of batting support from Mark Stacy, Jon Kertes, and Jim Mellinger. Stacy had three singles and 2 RBIs, Kertes had three RBIs on a triple and a single, and Mellinger had a double and a single and two RBIs. Freshwater didn't let up in the second game, scattering six singles to six different Morris Harvey batters as the Golden Eagles never seriously threatened. WLS plated its two runs in the third and six frames on a run-scoring double by Stacy and a triple by Lufft. Now 5-4 overall and 4-0 in the WVC, WLS takes a break from the diamond wars until a loop twinbill at Glenville State. MH *now stands 2-9 overall and 0-2 in the WVC.**

West Liberty 8 MH 0
(First Game)

| West Liberty | 8 runs | 14 hits | 2 errors |
| MH | 0 runs | 1 hit | 3 errors |

WL-Williams, WP (SO 9, W1)and DeSantis; Stacy 3S, 2 RBI; Kertes T, S, 3 RBI; DeSantis 2S; West 2S; Mellinger D, S, 2 RBI.

MH-Brown, LP (SO 7, W 4), Perry (5), Sweetnich (6), (SO2, W1), and Cappuccio; Given (sic) D.

West Liberty 2 MH 0
(Second Game)

| MH | 0 runs | 6 hits | 1 error |
| West Liberty | 2 runs | 4 hits | 2 errors |

MH-Woolwine, LP, (SO 4, W 3) and Donovan, six players with six singles.

WL-Freshwater, WP (SO7, W0), and DeSantis; Stacy D, RBI; Lufft T, RBI; West S; Schmidt S.

Riding a 4-1 record in the last five games, the first game of the twin bill went to the 'Toppers by a score of 8-0. As the April 11 issue of *The Trumpet* records it…

Dave Williams turned in a sparkling performance with an 8-0 triumph over Morris Harvey as he faced only 25 batters, four short of a perfect game. The senior, Coshocton, O., allowed only one hit while walking one and striking out seven. The Hilltoppers committed two errors. Kertes rapped a triple and a single, while Stacy had three singles. Jim Mellinger belted a double and a single and West and DeSantis had two singles. Girty, Lufft, and Frey each had a single.

In the second game, the same article goes on to say that...

WL downed Morris Harvey, 2-0, in the nightcap with Gary Freshwater picking up the win. Stacy had an RBI double and Schmidt had an RBI single. Lufft smacked a triple and West added another single.

Nozica's Golden Eagles would go on to finish the season 8-19 overall and 5-7 in the conference. Two players from the team, Ken Given, and pitcher, Steve Brown, would be members of the All-WVIAC team. The well-rounded Given would lead the team with a .346 batting average, including thirty hits, three doubles, three triples, 10 rbi's, and nine stolen bases. Brown would finish as the top pitcher on the team with a 5-2 record and a 1.23 ERA. In 52 1/3 innings, he would record 72 K's, save six games, while pitching three complete games. Brown would also record a two-hitter against Concord and a three-hit, 13-strikeout performance against the Yellow Jackets of West Virginia State. As a team, the Golden Eagles' biggest win of the '75 season would come against West Virginia University in a 2-1, 14-inning win five days after losing to the Hilltoppers.

After a short, two-day break, the Hilltoppers would once more hit the road for a doubleheader against a second team nicknamed the Pioneers. This time it was the Pioneers of Glenville State College.

Located in the town that gave the school its name, Glenville State College is a public college. The campus is situated half-way between Morgantown and Charleston, just off I-79, and a three-hour drive from the West Liberty campus. Established in 1872, the college boasts a student enrollment of nearly 1,400. Among its alumni is actor

Channing Tatum, who attended the school on a football scholarship but dropped out to pursue an acting career, and longtime college basketball official and 1980 graduate, Ted Valentine. The baseball team is coached by Bob Summers, who is in his first-year at Glenville.

Once more, wet conditions caused the game to be postponed on Saturday, April 5.

An article appearing in the April 7 edition of the *Wheeling News-Register* told a little of what lies ahead for the 'Toppers in the coming week…

If the weather cooperates, this figures to be a
busy week for West Liberty State's baseball
team. Coach Jim Watson's Hilltoppers are
scheduled to play four doubleheaders in six
days, beginning with a makeup twin bill at
Glenville today. Tomorrow will find Salem
coming to the WLSC campus, with West Virginia
University's baseballers due in on Friday and
West Liberty to play West Virginia State a pair
at Institute on Saturday. Watson doesn't feel
the schedule will be as taxing as it looks on his
four-deep starting pitching staff. He planned to
go with Ray Searage and Rick Bonar today,
coming back with Dave Williams and Gary
Freshwater in the Northern Division
confrontations with Salem tomorrow. That
would leave today's hurlers rested enough to
come back against WVU and Tuesday's duo
for the WVIC tilts on Saturday…

Saturday, April 7 vs. Glenville State College
(Overall record 5-4, Conference 4-0)

The weather conditions the day of the game were uncharacteristically cold and windy for that time in the

Glenville area. At 8:00am, the temperature was in the middle 20's with northwest winds gusting to 29mph. By the start of the first game at 1:00pm, the temps had risen to a windy 30 degrees.

In a brief, three-paragraph, seventeen-line article in the April 8 *Steubenville Herald-Star* entitled "West Liberty Extends Loop Mark to 6-0," the following notes the 'Toppers doubleheader with the Pioneers.

West Liberty State College's baseball team scored their third doubleheader sweep of the season as it beat Glenville State. The Hilltoppers hammered 14 hits in the opener, including home runs by Jon Kertes and Robbie Schmidt and four rbi's by Gary West. Pitcher Ray Searage gave up on two hits. Rick Bonar stifled on two hits in the nightcap. The run he needed came in the third singled when Mark Stacy and West doubled. West Liberty, 6-0 in the WVIC is scheduled to meet Salem College at home today...

"WLS Sweeps Glenville" is the title of an article that begins...

West Liberty State's baseball team rode a 14-hit hitting attack in the opener and the two-hit pitching effort of Rick Bonar in the nightcap Monday to sweep a W.Va. Conference twinbill from host Glenville State. The Hilltoppers routed the Pioneers in the front game by 15-1 but could get just four hits in the second game but they were enough to back Bonar's efforts in a 1-0 triumph. The wins were the fifth and sixth in succession for Coach Watson's team in the Conference. Glenville is now 1-3 in the league. There were plenty of hitting stars in the first

105

*game as Jon Kertes blasted a homer, a double,
and had four RBIs; Gary West had four RBI's
and had a triple and a single; and Robbie
Schmidt rifled a homer and added two singles.
Ray Searage went the route, breezing to the win
while allowing just two hits. It was West who
was the batting star in the second game, plating
Mark Stacy, who had three singles, with a
double in the third which was the only run of the
game. Ed Wilson of St. Marys took the hard
luck loss for the Pioneers. WLS doesn't have
much time for a breather, since the 'Toppers
return home today for a 1 p.m. twinbill with
Salem College.*

W. Liberty 15 Glenville 1
(First Game)

West Liberty	*15 runs*	*14 hits*	*0 errors*
Glenville	*1 run*	*2 hits*	*5 errors*

*WL-Searage WP (SO 8, W5)and DiSantis (sic), and
Spencer (5); Girty 2S; Kertes HR, D, 4rbi's; West T, S,
4rbi's; Schmidt HR, 2S; Lufft 2S.
G-Mathias (SO3 W2) LP, Lemmons (3) (SO1 W2), Bass
(4) (SO 0 W 1) and Rumer.*

Glenville 0 West Liberty 1
(Second Game)

Glenville	*0 runs*	*2 hits*	*2 errors*
West Liberty	*1 run*	*4 hits*	*2 errors*

*G-Wilson LP (SO 2 W2) and Reed
WL-Bonar WP (SO6, W6), and DiSantis (sic); Stacy 3S;
West D, rbi.*

As a young team comprised of eleven freshmen, twelve sophomores, one junior, and two seniors, the Pioneers would initially finish the season with three wins in eighteen games. But all that changed when it was discovered that one of the Pioneers players was academically ineligible. Consequently, the baseball team was forced to forfeit the three wins. The team ended the '75 season winless…0-18.

Of this, the school's newspaper, *The Glenville Mercury*, would write in a May 7 article that…

…the discovery of a Pioneer who was not carrying a significant number of hours to remain eligible for athletics, and, therefore, Glenville had to forfeit the three games they had won.

With two more conference victories in the win column, the Hilltoppers raised their record to 7-4 overall and an impressive 6-0 among conference opponents. Meanwhile, Coach Watson and his team return home to prepare for back-to-back doubleheaders with the Salem Tigers and the West Virginia University Mountaineers. The games with Salem would mark the 'Toppers fourth straight doubleheader.

———————

Salem College, at the time, a private school affiliated with the Seventh Day Adventists, was established in 1888 and began offering instruction a short, twelve months later. Located in the heart of its namesake city that provided the college its name, Salem, WV, the school lies a short hop-and-a-jump and a 20-minute drive to the west of the Bridgeport exit on I-79. The trip from Salem to West Liberty would traditionally take less than two hours. Although the school ranks near the bottom in numbers with the other ten WVIAC schools with just over 1,000 students, the school boasts impressive graduates and athletes. In addition to college football coaches Terry Bowden, Rich Rodriguez, and Jimbo Fisher, the school can also count among its graduates former West Virginia governor, Cecil Underwood, and former US Congressman and Senator Jennings Randolph. Having begun his baseball coaching career at the school in 1957, Clem Clower enters his eighteen-year of coaching the Tigers.

Saturday, April 5 vs. Salem College
(Overall record 7-4, Conference 6-0)
The Hilltoppers would enter the game with the Tigers not only riding a six-game winning streak but also posting seven wins in their last eight games. While the temperature at game time was 44 degrees, it came with much joy considering the temperature had risen some 20 degrees since 8:00am. Still, the skies were fair, with occasional wind gusts around 20mph. The cold weather produced cold bats as the 'Toppers would split the doubleheader with the Tigers, losing the first game in a shut-out 5-0, but returning to win the second game, 6-4. The first-game defeat would be the Hilltoppers' first conference loss of the '75 season.

With a lead entitled "Diamondmen Show High Rankings in NAIA," Don Billham, Associate Sports Editor for *The Trumpet*, writes in a Friday, April 18 article that...

...Tom Fitzgerald allowed only one hit, that by
Tom Lufft, in turning back the 'Toppers 5-0 in
the front game of a twinbill with Salem,
Tuesday, April 8.
In the nightcap, Gary Freshwater allowed only
four hits and fanned seven in a 6-4 victory.
Rob Schmidt hit a three-run homer and added
two singles, while Gregg DeSantis had three
hits and Stan Duplaga had two to supply the
plate power...

Of the split with Salem, an article entitled "Salem, WLS Split Pair," would report...
Salem College routed West Liberty State's

*pitching ace Dave Williams for five runs in
the second inning of the first game Tuesday
as the Hilltoppers and the Tigers split a West
Virginia Conference doubleheader on the
WLS diamond. Salem handed the 'Toppers a
5-0 setback in the opener for West Liberty's first
loss of the year but the hosts rebounded for
three runs in the sixth frame of the nightcap for
a 6-4 triumph and the twinbill split. The split
makes West Liberty's WVC mark 7-1 on the
year while the Hilltoppers' overall record is 8-5.
Salem is 3-3 in league play. West Liberty
managed just one hit in the front game, a fourth
inning single by freshman Tom Lufft, though
Williams held the Tigers to just four bingles.
The 'Toppers did pound out 12 hits in the
second game, including the game-deciding
blow in the sixth, a three-run homer by
Wheeling's Robbie Schmidt. Catcher Greg
(sic) DeSantis had three singles and scored two
runs.*

"First League Loss for West Liberty" reads the headline
in the April 9 edition of the *Wheeling News-Register*.
*After sustaining its first West Virginia
Intercollegiate Conference baseball defeat of
the spring in a home doubleheader split with
Salem College yesterday afternoon, West Liberty
takes a couple days off before hosting West
Virginia University in a twin bill on Friday
starting at 1:00 p.m....Now 7-1 in loop play and
8-5 overall, West Liberty got only one hit off the
Tigers' Fitzgerald, who struck out six and walked
three, in losing a 5-0 nod in the opener. The
lone safety was a single by freshman shortstop*

Dr. Michael F. Price

*Tom Lufft in the fourth inning. Salem managed
only four hits but got to right-handed ace Dave
Williams for all five runs in the second inning.
Some lose play on the reult (sic) of the
Hilltoppers, who had seven errors in the twin
bill, aided the rally. In the second game,
winning pitcher Gary Freshwater and reliever
Mark Fabbro combined on a four-hitter in a
6-4 triumph. Coach Jim Watson's club collected
12 hits but had to erase a 3-2 Salem lead by
scoring three times in the sixth inning on Robbie
Schmidt's home run with two mates on base.
Greg (sic) DeSantis rapped out three singles
and scored a pair of runs while Shawn Girty
and Stan Duplaga had two hits each for the
winners...*

W. Liberty 0 Salem 5
(First Game)

Salem	5 runs	4 hits	0 errors
West Liberty	0 runs	1 hit	3 errors

S-Fitzgerald, WP (SO6, W2) and Ciccorelli; Viehdorfer
S, 2 RBI; Brown S, 2 RBI.
WL-Williams, LP, (SO 7, W2) and DeSantis; Lufft, S.

W. Liberty 6 Salem 4
(Second Game)

West Liberty	6 runs	12 hits	4 errors
Salem	4 runs	4 hits	1 error

WL-Freshwater, WP (SO7, W4), Fabbro (6) (SO1, W0),
and DeSantis; Girty D, S; DeSantis 2S, 2 runs; Schmidt
HR, 3 RBI, 2 S; Duplaga D, S.
S-Brady, LP (SO3, W6), Venderlich (6), (SO, W2) and
Ciccorelli; Brown 2S, 2 RBI; Holman D, 2 RBI.

A doubleheader split means that the Hilltoppers record now stands at 7-1 in conference games and 8-5 overall. Next up for the Hilltoppers will be West Virginia University and a rematch of a doubleheader that took place at the close of fall ball. The two teams split the practice game with the 'Toppers winning the first game 4-3 and losing the nightcap 7-6 in 10-innings.

As the largest of all the schools in the state, West Virginia University has a student enrollment of nearly 18,000. Founded as a public institution in 1867 as part of the Morrill Land Grant Act, its main campus is located in Morgantown. Since the 1980s, the school has appeared regularly on the list of the Top 10 Party Schools in America. Among the school's noted alumni include NBA great Jerry West, and TV star, Don Knotts. Dale Ramsburg is the head coach of the Mountaineers and is in his eighth year with the team. The team ended the previous year with a 12-13 record.

"Young Hilltop Hurlers to Face Mountaineers" reads the lead in the April 10 edition of the *Wheeling News-Register*.
West Liberty State baseball skipper Jim Watson
is expected to throw two young hurlers at West
Virginia University in tomorrow afternoon's
home doubleheader which begins at 1 p.m.
Lefty Ray Searage and righty (sic) Rick Bonar,
who pitched in Monday's twin bill sweep over
Glenville State, will get the call against the 3-8
record of the Mountaineers who were slated to
play at Waynesburg today. With another
conference twin bill scheduled against West
Virginia State at Institute on Saturday, Watson
isn't planning on using veterans Dave Williams
and Gary Freshwater until then…Tuesday's
split with Salem on the home diamond saw a

111

Dr. Michael F. Price

six-game win streak end for the Hilltoppers...

Friday, April 11 vs. West Virginia University
(Overall record 8-5, Conference 7-1)
The cold temperatures continued to hang around on the day of the game. When the first pitch was delivered at 1:00pm, it was 46 degrees. This seemed a tremendous improvement from five hours earlier when the temperature was a chilly 29 degrees. A steady wind out of the North and Northwest and partly cloudy skies remained throughout the game. In the end, the 'Toppers would lose both games to the Mountaineers, 8-6 and 5-4.

Of the game, Associate Sports Editor for *The Trumpet,* Don Billham, notes in a Friday, April 18 article that...

...Against West Virginia, the 'Toppers were
turned back twice, 8-6 and 5-4. Gary West had
a three-run homer, John Curtis (sic) added a
circuit blast and a single, and Rob Schmidt had
two hits in the first game. In the second,
Schmidt put the ball out of the park for the
fourth time this season. Ed Dulkowski (sic) was
tagged for both losses in relief.

The Mountaineers would finish the season 10-18.

As many of the teams of the WVIAC reach the half-way point in their spring schedule, an article in the April 18 edition of *The Trumpet*, written by Don Billham, Associate Sports Editor, leads with the byline "Diamondmen Show High Ranking in NAIA," states...

Coach Watson's diamondmen...show some high
rankings in recently released NAIA baseball
statistics. Junior hurler Gary Freshwater, with
a 4-0 slate, is ranked eighth in earned run
average with a .077 mark. Rick Bonar, who is

112

2-1, is tied for 12th in ERA with a 1.01 reading,
and the WLS staff is fourth in the NAIA in ERA
at 2.04. Power-hitting first baseman Rob
Schmidt has stroked five home runs to place
him in a six-way tie for fifth in that category.
Schmidt also leads the team with a .315 batting
average and is second in hits, with 17, and runs
batted in, 14. Mark Stacy leads the squad in
hits at 19, while John Curtis (sic) is first in runs
scored and in RBI's, 15. Also aiding in the
cause at the plate are Gregg DeSantis, hitting
at a .296 clip with 16 hits, and Stan Duplaga,
with a team-leading five doubles and a .270
average. Overall, the Hilltoppers have a
higher batting average than their opponents,
.265 to .189, ad have outhit the opposition 134
to 89. Dave Williams is leading the mound
staff with 33 strikeouts in 43 innings, while
Freshwater has 25 whiffs in 26 innings pitched...

When the team arrived home from the spring trip, and now, the Hilltoppers had logged just over 1,400 miles and ridden in school vans nearly twenty-four hours in total. These numbers are in addition to the physical and emotional challenges of playing in three doubleheaders and a single, nine-inning game. Despite losing three of the last four games and giving up eighteen runs while scoring only ten, the 'Toppers are looking forward to the second half of the schedule. Ironically, the 'Toppers would find themselves in the first several days of April in the same situation as in the early days of March...gathered in the school vans on the way to an away game. Needless to say, the team seemed ready to tackle the remaining games on the schedule, starting with the April 12 game with the Yellow Jackets of West Virginia State College.

Located a short, 10-minute drive south of Charleston, West Virginia State College was established in 1891 as another of the nineteen public colleges that grew out of the Morrill Land Grant Act of 1862. WV State is considered one of the Historically Black College and Universities in the US. It boasts of student enrollment of just over 2,800. Among the school's alumni is Katherine G. Johnson, NASA mathematician, and the lead character in the movie *Hidden Figures*. The Yellow Jackets are coached by Bob Maxwell, who is in his fifth-year at the school.

Saturday, April 12 vs. West Virginia State College
(Overall record 8-7, Conference 7-1)
On a mostly cloudy day with temperatures at the first pitch in the low-40s and wind gusts during the second game reaching over 20mph, it should come as no surprise that by the last out of the second game, the temperature had risen a meager 4 degrees. Just as the team had done four days earlier in the doubleheader with Salem College, the Hilltoppers would follow the same path with the Yellow Jackets, losing the first game but coming back in the second game to salvage a split. The scores were 5-2 and 3-1, respectively.

With a headline that reads "Hilltoppers Get Twin Bill Split," the *Steubenville Herald-Star* shared that...

The Hilltoppers...edged West Virginia State
3-1, after losing the first game 5-2, at the State
Field. Rick Spencer, a pinch runner from
Steubenville, scored the winning run on a single
by Rich Frey in the seventh inning of the
nightcap. Gary Freshwater was the winning
pitcher. In the opener, Follansbee's Greg (sic)
DeSantis socked a run-scoring triple and a
single for the Hilltoppers.

The Season That Was

In the April 18 issue of *The Trumpet*, Associate Sports Editor, Don Billham, records that...

...West Liberty split a two-game set with W.Va State, losing 5-2 in the front game, and coming back to take the second, 2-1. Gregg DeSantis had two of the Hilltoppers six hits with a triple and a single, as Dave Williams was handed his third setback of the year. Freshwater came back in game two with a seven-hit, six-strikeout performance to nail down his fourth win. Schmidt blasted his fifth home run of the spring and added a single to pace the attack.

In an April 13 article appearing in the *Wheeling News-Register* with the headline "W. Liberty In Split," the following appears...

Freshman Rich Frey singled home pinch runner Rick Spencer with the winning run in the bottom of the seventh inning giving West Liberty a 2-1 victory and a split in Saturday's West Virginia Conference doubleheader with West Virginia State at Institute. After dropping the first game 5-2, the Hilltoppers came back in the second game behind the pitching of Gary Freshwater who gave up only one unearned run to record the victory. Rob Schmidt put West Liberty ahead 1-0 in the fourth inning on a 400-ft. home run before State countered with a run in the top of the sixth, setting up the Hilltoppers' last inning heroics.

In the day's first contest, the hosts scored three runs in the opening frame off Dave Williams and added single runs in the fourth and fifth to notch the triumph. Greg (sic) DeSantis had a run scoring triple and a single for West Liberty. The

Dr. Michael F. Price

*Hilltoppers who were playing their fourth
doubleheader this week, now have a 9-8 overall
mark and are in first place in the conference's
Northern Division with an 8-2 record....*

The 'Toppers have three non-conference and four conference games remaining.

Following six games and 42-innings of baseball over eight days, including a 6-hour, nearly 400-mile round trip journey to play West Virginia State College, the 'Toppers were ready to move on for battle with their next conference foe...the Bobcats of West Virginia Wesleyan College.

As a private college established by the United Methodist Church in 1890, West Virginia Wesleyan College is located approximately forty miles southeast of Clarksburg in Buckhannon. Taking its place as one of a handful of colleges in the US with the word "Wesleyan" in the school's title, the name was chosen in honor of the founder of Methodism, Charles Wesley. In terms of the student population, the enrollment is nearly 1,650, which places it sixth in size among the ten colleges that comprise the WVIAC. Among the more noted Wesleyan alumni is Ted Cassidy...better known as "Lurch" of The Addams Family. The Bobcats are coached by Hank Ellis.

"Showdown Time for the Hilltoppers" reads the headline in the April 15 issue of the Wheeling News-Register.
*Showdown time has arrived for West Liberty
State's defending West Virginia Intercollegiate
Conference champions as they entertain
Northern Division rival West Virginia Wesleyan
for a pair of games tomorrow starting at 1 p.m.
Both teams have two losses to date against*

116

conference opposition, but the Hilltoppers have the better rating with an 8-2 mark and a 100.00 average to 6-2 for the Bobcats and a 96.2 rating. Coach Jim Watson has his right-handed aces Dave Williams and Gary Freshwater ready to go in the twin bill. While only 1-3 this season, Williams has been the victim of some tough luck and he still sports a fine 2.12 ERA along with 33 strikeouts in 43 innings of pitching. Freshwater, the former Brooke High hurler, has a perfect 4-0 , mark to date, including a sharp 0.77 ERA and 25 strikeouts in 26 innings. Control has been a big factor in Freshwater's success this season as he has given up just 10 walks. Also sporting a winning record for West Liberty, which has an overall record of 9-8, is sophomore Rick Bonar, who is 2-1, with a 1.01 ERA. The Hilltoppers' team ERA is 2.04... Following tomorrow's pair with Wesleyamn (sic), the Hilltoppers journey to Fairmont State on Saturday for another double dip...

Wednesday, April 16 vs. West Virginia Wesleyan College (Overall record 9-8, Conference 8-2)

With partly cloudy skies, winds gusts as much as 25mph, and shifting winds throughout...first from the WNW, then from the NNW, and finally from the West...it's little wonder that the temperature had risen from the first pitch of the two-game series to the last out, a scant 5 degrees! Still, the temperature in the mid-'50s was a welcome feeling. In the end, the 'Toppers would sweep the Bobcats 6-0 and 7-1, making this the fifth conference doubleheader win of the season for West Liberty.

Dr. Michael F. Price

With a headline that reads "West Liberty Victor Twice in Loop Play," the *Steubenville Herald-Star* of April 17 records...

> *West Liberty State College upped its conference record...turning back West Virginia Wesleyan 6-0 and 7-1. The host 'Toppers were benefitted by two fine one hit performances by Dave Williams and Gary Freshwater. In the first game won by Williams, West Liberty pounded out eight hits with Greg (sic) DeSantis rapping two singles. Kertes, Stacy, and West had doubles while Mellinger added a triple. The nightcap saw Freshwater sparkle on the mound while Jim (sic) Schmidt contributed a home run. Girty, Mellinger, and Duplaga had two singles each for the winners...The one hit off Freshwater, former Brooke High baseball standout, was a homer in the fifth inning by Mike Price. The Hilltoppers supported Freshwater with 11 hits.*

Of the win, *The Trumpet* edition of April 25 would chronicle that...

> *Dave Williams and Gary Freshwater hurled one-hitters' to lead the Gold and Black to a 6-0 and 7-1 sweep of the Wesleyan's Bobcats Wednesday April 16 at home. Williams fanned seven and yielded only a fifth inning single in the opener to raise his record to 2-3 and lower his ERA to 2.17. Rob Schmidt blasted a three-run homer, the first of two he had in the wins, Gregg DeSantis went two-for-three, Jon Kertes, Mark Stacy and Gary West had doubles, and Jim Mellinger stroked a triple to lead the eight-hit attack. In the nightcap, Freshwater struck*

118

*out seven and allowed only a fifth inning home
run by Mike Price upping his glittering mark to
5-0. Schmidt's second circuit blast of the day,
Shawn Girty's two singles, and two hits apiece
by Stan Duplaga and Jim Mellinger paced an
11-hit 'Topper surge.*

"West Liberty Nears Pennant" reads the headlines in the
April 17 edition of the *Wheeling News-Register*. The article
goes on to say…

*Command pitching performances Wednesday
by right-handers Dave Williams and Gary
Freshwater moved West Liberty State to the
threshold of a fourth straight Northern Division
baseball championship in the West Virginia
Intercollegiate Conference. While it's too early
to pop the champagne corks or toss head coach
Jim Watson into the showers, the back-to-back
one-hitters served up in a doubleheader sweep
of West Virginia Wesleyan on the home
diamond have the Hilltoppers within easy
striking distance of a berth in the WVIC best-of
-three playoff against the Southern Division
winner on May 10-11 at Watt Powell Park in
Charleston. West Liberty is now 10-2 in league
play and 11-8 overall. The Bobcats were the
closest rivals to Watson's young but talented
team prior to yesterday's double dip, which
dropped Wesleyan to 6-4 in league play. Only
six games remain against conference opponents
for the Hilltoppers, including a doubleheader
at Fairmont Saturday at 1 p.m. Williams, who
tossed a no-hitter last season against West
Virginia Tech, worked into the fifth yesterday
before surrendering a bloop hit and went on*

*from there to post a 6-0 triumph, striking out
seven and walking five for his second win in
five decisions this spring. Robbie Schmidt,
whose bat has been on fire since early in the
campaign, smacked a three-run homer in the
third to give the hosts a 4-0 lead. Greg (sic)
DeSantis had two of the eight hits picked up by
West Liberty. The Hilltoppers came back with a
14-hit onslaught in the second game, featuring
still another homer by Schmidt, his eighth of the
spring and fourth in the last six contests.
Shawn Girty, Jim Mellinger and Stan Duplaga
contributed two hots each. Freshwater, former
Brooke athlete who now sports a perfect 5-0
record, also carried his no-hit bid into the fifth
when Mike Price slammed a home run. But the
decision was safely tucked away by then as a
two-run first and a five-run outburst in the
second led to an easy 7-1 WLSC triumph.*

W. Va. Wesleyan 0 West Liberty 6
(First Game)

WV Wesleyan   0 runs   1 hit   0 errors
West Liberty   6 runs   8 hit   0 errors
   *Batteries: Lavin, Massey (4) and Williams; Williams and
   DeSantis.*

W. Liberty 7 W. Va. Wesleyan 0
(Second Game)

West Liberty   7 runs   11 hits   1 error
WV Wesleyan   1 run   1 hit   1 error
   *Batteries: Freshwater and DeSantis; Carroll, Kropa (2)
   and Williams.*

With first place in the Northern Division on-the-line, Fresh remembers the two-game series as a heated one, especially the second game.

...We were battling for first place and we won the first game. I started the second. I remember them yelling and getting on me like crazy from their dugout, trying to rattle me. I got fired up and started striking guys out with nothing but fastballs. Greg (sic) DeSantis would show the ball in the hitter's face after each strikeout before throwing around the infield. Watson kept saying, "we will not be intimidated on our home field!" Anyway, I had a no hitter in the fifth, grooved a fastball, and the guy hit a home run. I remember him saying, "there goes your no-hitter, there goes your shut out too," as he rounded second. Ended up with a one-hitter. By the way, the guy that hit the home run, his name was Mike Price!

In passing, it must be noted that the reference to Mike Price hitting a home run is not a typo. There was actually a player on the Wesleyan team with the name Mike Price. According to open records that go back all the way to his first days playing baseball, West Liberty's Mike Price, aka Piney/the Woodsman, never hit a round-tripper in college, high school, or in little league. The only time he may have hit a home run was in whiffle ball games with his brothers Frank, Rodney, and David…and in his dreams.

Equally interesting that day was the horoscope for Fresh, born under the zodiac sign of Leo, the bull, which would read in part…

Individuals…have profound, sensitive emotions and a tendency to take things quite personally.

———————

121

The Hilltoppers were greeted by some good news from an article that appeared in *The Trumpet* on April 25, was entitled "Baseball Team Leads WVIC Northern Division."

The Hilltoppers, 11-8 overall and 10-2 in the conference, held a commanding lead in the Northern Division... "West Liberty held a 22.5 point-average over second-place Salem and needed only four wins in the last six league games to wrap up the crown. Point averages are figured by dividing the number of games played into total points, which are awarded on a 100-point basis for victories and an additional 10 points for every win chalked up by a defeated opponent...

North Division

West Liberty	*10-2*	*117.5*
Salem	*6-4*	*95.0*
WV Wesleyan	*6-4*	*89.0*
Fairmont	*5-5*	*73.0*
A-B	*4-4*	*70.0*

South Division

Concord	*6-4*	*81.0*
WV State	*5-5*	*75.0*
WV Tech	*5-5*	*71.0*
M. Harvey	*3-5*	*62.0*
Davis & Elkins	*4-10*	*41.4*

First baseman Robbie Schmidt upped his team-leading batting average to 322. He also leads the squad in roundtrippers, with eight, and runs batted in, 19, while placing second in hits with 19. Mark Stacy has 21 bingles to lead in that category and shows a .300 average. DeSantis is second in the average column at .311, while Mellinger is third at .302. Kertes is hitting at a .278 clip with three doubles, three triples, three homers and 16 RBI's, and Girty, batting .265, has stolen 13 bases. Overall, the Hilltoppers have raised the team batting average to a respectable .276. Freshwater leads the mound staff with five wins and has a 1.08 ERA, while showing 32 strikeouts in 33 innings pitched. Rick Bonar, 2-1 with a 1.26 ERA, and Williams, at 2.17, are also under the staff ERA of 2.28 Williams leads the group with 40 whiffs in 50 innings pitched...

———————

Following a short, two-day break, the Hilltoppers would then play three doubleheaders in 4-days, all away games, beginning with a 90-mile, 90-minute trip down I-79 to play the Fairmont Fighting Falcons.

———————

Fairmont State College was established in 1865, making it the second oldest public college in the state; only West Liberty is older. Just as several other colleges mentioned within the pages of this book adopted their name from the city surrounding the campus, including California State (PA), Davis and Elkins, Glenville State, Salem, and West Liberty, Fairmont State College did the same. Located half-way between Morgantown and Clarksburg on I-79, the student enrollment of FSC is just over 3,000, making it the largest school among the eleven schools of the WVIAC. While the city of Fairmont has the honor of being called the home of Olympic gymnast Mary Lou Retton and the birthplace of the pepperoni roll, the college counts among its alumni Herbert Morrison, the radio reporter whose voice is heard describing the disaster of the Hindenburg in 1937, and Bill Stewart, former head football coach of the West Virginia Mountaineers.

According to the schedule, the game was initially to be played on Saturday, April 19, but had to be postponed. In a *Wheeling News-Register* article of April 20 with the byline "Toppers Face Back-to-Back Doubleheaders"...

West Liberty State College's baseball team faces West Virginia Intercollegiate Conference doubleheaders this week. The Hilltoppers will try and makeup Saturday's twin bill postponement with Fairmont State tomorrow on the Fighting Falcons diamond and then go to Philippi on Tuesday to face Alderson-Broaddus. Starting times both days will be 1 p.m. A sweep on (sic) of the next four games would clinch a fourth straight Northern Division championship for Coach Jim Watson's Hilltoppers, who are 11-8 overall and boast a 10-2 conference mark. Pitchers Monday for Coach Watson's club will be lefty Ray Searage and righty (sic) Rick Bonar. Righthanders Dave Williams and Gary Freshwater will work on Tuesday against A-B.

Monday, April 21 vs. Fairmont State College
(Overall record 11-8, Conference 10-2)

In one sense, the 2-game conference series with the Falcons was typical. The area temperature at the start of the 1:00pm doubleheader was in the high 50's. It remained there throughout the day, thanks to cloudy skies and wind gusts from West and Southwest, at one point reaching 30mph. In another sense, it was business as usual for the 'Toppers on the field as the team swept Fairmont 12-3 and 2-1.

"Hilltoppers Take Pair," the article from the April 22 edition of the *Wheeling News-Register* begins…

…Tom Lufft hit two home runs and collected four RBI's to lead a 13-hit attack as West Liberty rolled to a 12-3 triumph in the opener. Rob Schmidt continued his long ball hitting as he knocked a three-run homer and also had four RBI's in the first game. Ray Searage got the win as he allowed only four hits and struck out seven. The Hilltoppers rode the four-hit pitching of Rick Bonar to a 2-1 win in the second game as the ex-River High athlete fanned 10 batters. Jim Watson's team got both its runs in the third inning as Shawn Girty tripled home a run and Mark Stacy singles in Girty.

In a related piece that reads "Hilltoppers Sweep Two Off Fairmont," the article goes on to say…

…Tom Lufft belted two roundtrippers and team leader Rob Schmidt added one as the two sluggers divided eight runs batted in including three-run homers by each. In the nightcap, ex-River High athlete Rick Bonar struck out 10 Falcons as WLS made two runs in the third inning stand up. Ex-Steubenville Big Red Mark Stacy, who had a double and a single in the opener, knocked in the deciding run after ex-St. Clairsville High stand-out Shawn Girty tripled in the first run.*

W. Liberty 12 Fairmont 3
(First Game)

West Liberty	12 runs	13 hits	1 error
Fairmont	3 runs	4 hits	1 error

WL-Searage (SO7, W4), and DeSantis, Spencer (6), Lufft 2 HRs, 4 RBI's; Schmidt 3-run HR; Stacy D, S; Kertes 2S
F-Book (SO3, 4W), O'Neil (6), (SO1, W1), and Wilburn, Kupets HR, Gallagher 2-run HR

Fairmont 1 W. Liberty 2
(Second Game)

Fairmont	1 run	4 hits	0 errors
West Liberty	2 runs	7 hits	1 error

    F-Riffle (SO2, 0W) and Wilburn, Kupets 2S
    WL-Bonar (SO10, W2), and DeSantis, Girty T, RBI; Stacy winning RBI

Because of the rainout on April 19 with Fairmont, the Monday, April 21, game with California State College was moved to Monday, April 28. Next up for the Hilltoppers is a scheduled conference game with Alderson-Broaddus.

As a private college that emerged from a union between two Baptists institutions, Alderson-Broaddus College traces its roots as far back as 1871, with the establishment of Broaddus Institute. Following a move West from Winchester, VA, to Clarksburg, WV, in the later years of the Reconstruction Era of American History, the school moved once again, this time settling due east of Clarksburg in the town of Philippi in the latter years of the first decade of the 20th century. The school changed its name to Broaddus College during the first World War. Alderson College was founded in Alderson, WV, at the turn of the 20th century. With each school facing financial challenges in the years leading up to the Depression, the schools merged, creating Alderson-Broaddus College, in Philippi. A-B is one of the smallest of the WVIAC schools, and is a 2-hour, 120-mile drive from West Liberty. While the school is a 'dry school" (no alcohol allowed on campus), A-B may be best known as the first school in the U.S. to offer a four-year physician's assistant program. One of the earliest battles of the Civil War took place in Philippi; consequently, the school goes by the nickname of the Battlers, with the mascot named Skirmish. The head baseball coach is Jack Funk, who is in his 10th year at A-B. His team comes into the game with WL 7-3 overall and 6-2 in conference play.

In an article entitled "Battler Baseball Team Is Off To A Good Start," sports writer John Dooley, writing in the A-B newspaper, *The Columns*, on April 18, comments on the upcoming game versus the 'Toppers, by saying...

Going into the double header with Glenville,
Sat., April 12, the Battlers stood at 3-1 in
conference play and 4-2, overall. The 3-1 mark
put Coach Jack Funk's men at the top of the
WVIAC, and tied with West Liberty and West
Virginia Wesleyan...Next Tuesday could prove
to be the day of showdown as the local field
will be the sight of the A-B – West Liberty
double-notcher. The Hilltoppers are the
defending WVIAC champions and are
generally picked to be the team to beat...

Tuesday, April 22 vs. Alderson-Broaddus College
(Overall 13-8, Conference 12-2)

At game time, the temperature was in the mid-60s, with partly cloudy skies and little wind. The weather conditions played an insignificant role as the 'Toppers split the doubleheader with the Battlers, winning the first game 5-1 while losing the nightcap 6-5.

"West Liberty in Split," reads the headline in the April 23 edition of the *Wheeling News Register*. The article goes on to say...

Invading West Liberty State College found the
Alderson-Broaddus baseball team difficult to

Dr. Michael F. Price

*handle Tuesday afternoon but a 6-5 comeback
nod in the nightcap gave the Hilltoppers a split
in the West Virginia Intercollegiate Conference
doubleheader and a virtual lock on a fourth
straight Northern Division championships...
Heavy hitting by Terry Johnson and the four-hit
pitching of Steve Lesser gave the Battlers a 5-1
verdict over WLSC in yesterday's opener. It
marked the second straight year that Lesser has
gone the distance to beat the Gold and Black.
Johnson stroked a home run and a single while
knocking in three runs as Alderson-Broaddus
handed senior Dave Williams his fourth loss in
six decisions. Robbie Schmidt stroked a pair of
singles to collect half the Hilltopper hits off
Lesser. In the nightcap, Johnson hit another
homer as A-B vaulted to an early 2-0 lead.
After West had gone in front by 5-2, Tom
Camasso blasted a three-run homer in the top
of the seventh to tie it up. West Liberty got the
winning run in the last of the seventh as Mark
Stacy singled and later scored on another
single by freshman shortstop Tom Lufft.
Lufft had a pair of singles and two RBI's in the
nightcap, while also with two hits were Stacy,
Schmidt and Jim Mellinger. Shawn Girty
stroked a bases-loaded triple to drive on three
runs during a four-run Hilltopper outburst in
the bottom of the fourth. Winning pitcher was
surprise started Mark Fabbro, the freshman
from Oak Glen who went all the way and gave
up six hits. Fabbro whiffed three and had one
strikeout to even his record at 1-1.*

The Battlers would win three more times in their next seven games and end the season 13-6 overall and 12-5 in the conference. After starting out 8-0 in conference play, the Hilltoppers would now stand 13-3.

With yet another doubleheader split, the second in the past five games, the Hilltoppers would return to the diamond for the last scheduled game of the month, a doubleheader with local opponent, Steubenville College.

Of the ten non-conference colleges on the Hilltoppers '75 schedule, Steubenville College is one of the youngest, established in 1946. The private, Catholic school was founded to serve the educational needs of not only local students but veterans from WW II. While the city is named after Baron von Steuben, an American military officer during the Revolutionary War, the college adopted its name after the city. A short, 35-minute drive from the WL campus, the more notable residents who once called the city of Steubenville their home include former pro football player Danny Abramowicz, former major league pitcher Rollie Fingers, ESPN announcer John Buccigross, and actor and entertainer Dean Martin. Among the school's alumni are Princess Alexandra of Luxembourg, and her young brother, Prince Sebastien.

Saturday, April 26 vs. College of Steubenville
(Overall 14-9, Conference 13-3)
Rained out.

Next up for the 'Toppers is a short, one-hour drive to southcentral Pennsylvania and a non-conference doubleheader at California State College.

Located along the banks of the Monongahela River, one of the few rivers in America that flows North, the campus of

Dr. Michael F. Price

California State College is surrounded by the city of California, Pennsylvania. Established in 1852, the public college of nearly 4,300 students makes CSC not only the second oldest school the Hilltoppers have on the schedule but also the second-largest school in terms of enrollment that the 'Toppers will play. Among the school's alumni are Bruce Del Canton, former major league pitcher, Frank Mascara, former US Congressman, and Shaka Smart, current head coach of the University of Texas men's basketball team. In 1974, the Vulcans finished the season at an even .500...13-13...while splitting the two-game series with the Hilltoppers losing the first game 8-7 and winning the nightcap, 6-2. The Vulcans come into the game with the Hilltoppers with a 9-5 record, including a doubleheader loss to the West Virginia Mountaineers on April 13 that saw the teams combine for 45-runs in the two-game slugfest! Senior first-baseman, and second-team all NAIA District 18 all-star selection in 1974, Dom Lombardo, leads the team. In addition, Lombardo was second in the nation in 1974 with 12 doubles in 26 games (= a double every other game).

In his 16th season at the helm is coach Mitch Bailey.

Monday, April 28 vs. California State College (PA)
(Overall record 14-9, Conference 13-3)

At 8:00am on game day, the temperature was 51 degrees. By game time, the temperature had risen only slightly with partly cloudy skies and light winds. The 'Toppers would be shut out in the first game 4-0 while losing the second game 12-11.

In an article in *The California Times* of Friday, May 2, along with a headline of "Vulcans in First Place," sportswriter Dave Gentile writes...

For the first time since the state conference in
baseball was formed, the California State
College Vulcans finds themselves in first place

*with a perfect 6-0 record. The Vulcans are 11-7
overall and 8-4 in District 18 competition.
Slippery Rock, Clarion, and West Liberty
represent the last six Vulcan victories, all of
which were in the form of doubleheader sweeps.
...Monday against West Liberty the Vulcans
fought off Mother Nature and the West Liberty
team, sweeping the doubleheader 3-0 and 12-11.
The big surprise of the six-straight victories
wasn't the explosive bats of the Vulcans.
Everyone knew they could hit. But rather it was
the unexpected fine performance by the Vulcans
newest addition to the pitching staff, Gregg
Fussel. Fussel, who has been a reserve catcher
and outfielder all year was called to take on
some mound chores Monday. He accepted the
challenge and came thought more than anyone
could have dreamed: holding West Liberty to
only two runs in the last five innings, after the
Vulcans fell behind 9-0. Fussel's performance
enabled the Vulcans to come from behind in
extraordinary fashion to dispose of the West
Liberty team 12-11.*

"Hilltopper Lose 2" was the lead in an article that
appeared in the April 29 edition of the *Wheeling News-
Register*, saying…

*West Liberty State blew a 9-0 lead and then saw
host California State come up with the winning
run in the bottom of the eighth to gain a
doubleheader sweep over the Hilltoppers
Monday afternoon by scores of 4-0 and
12-11. Coach Jim Watson's team was limited
to four hits in the opener by Vulcan hurler Greg
Sporovatch with Olombardo (sic) knocking a*

home run and LaBrasca two singles to spark the host's attack. In the second game, the Hilltoppers scored six runs in the first inning and three in the second but couldn't hold off California which came back with seven tallies in its half of the second, eventually knotting the score in the seventh and winning with a single run in the first extra inning. Jim Mellinger paced West Liberty in the nightcap with three RBI's while Tom Lufft and Stan Duplaga added two each. West Liberty, which is now 15-11 overall, will entertain West Virginia Tech in a conference game Saturday.

Batteries for West Liberty for the first game were Freshwater and DeSantis. Ray Searage was the starter in the second game but was relieved in the second inning by Rick Bonar. Mark Fabbro entered the game in the fifth, with Rick Spencer handling the catching duties.

The Vulcans would end the '75 season with a 16-12 record.

With little time to reflect on the six losses over the last 12 games, including doubleheader sweeps at WVU and CSC, and splits with Salem and West Virginia State, the Hilltoppers began looking ahead to the four final games of the '75 season.

WL's non-conference and conference record the first fifteen days of April mirrors the team's record for the last fifteen days. Between April 1–15, the 'Toppers overall record stood at 6-4 and 6-2 in conference games. The team had doubleheader wins at Morris Harvey and Glenville State while splitting doubleheaders with Salem College and West

Virginia State. The two additional Hilltopper losses during the period came at the hands of non-conference foe, West Virginia University. From April 16 to the end of the month, the 'Toppers overall record stands at 5-3. Included in the win column is a conference, doubleheader win against West Virginia Wesleyan and Fairmont, and a two-game split with Alderson Broaddus. A two-game sweep at the hands of non-conference California State College and a single loss to fellow conference member Alderson-Broaddus accounts for the 'Toppers three losses during the final two weeks of April.

Beyond baseball, the month of April included a variety of on-and-off campus activities. Around 50 members of second-year dental hygienists, including Christie Derrow and Janice Propchek, made a trip to Cambridge State Hospital, OH, on April 11 to gain practical experience treating mental patients, alcoholics, and drug addicts. As Robbie Schmidt was sitting with the committee planning Greek Week activities, his baseball teammate, Rich Frey, was doing all he could to help the Hilltoppers bowling team defeat Glenville in a one-day roll-off for first place in the conference. Despite finishing the playoff by knocking down nearly 1,100 pins and scoring a high game 241, the team lost to Glenville. The 36-member Newark Boys Choir performed in College Hall on Monday, April 14, while the movie for Friday, April 18, is *The Getaway*, starring Steve McQueen and Ali MacGraw. Just as a host of volunteers from campus were preparing to welcome athletes from around the area as part of the Special Olympics competition at the school on April 26, the Hilltop Players were closing the year with a rousing rendition of *Jesus Christ, Superstar*. With over seventy cast members, including a full orchestra, the show ran for an impressive five nights. Finally, it seems that several players on the baseball team wanted to submit the names of no less than ten teammates into the "Ugly Man on Campus" contest being sponsored by Delta Chi fraternity. However, the idea was scrubbed when the players discovered the winning prize was a mere two kegs of beer.

'Ugly Man' Contest Is Wednesday Night

As the calendar turns from April to May, and the Hilltoppers prepare to play the last four regular-season games of the '75 schedule, the travel is all but complete. The remaining games will be played at a more relaxed pace…four games…both doubleheaders…over nine days… ending with a non-conference tilt with Frostburg State (MD) on May 7, and two games against conference foe West Virginia Tech.

Inning 9 (May 1975)

Baseball is a great game
because anything can happen thru the ninth inning.
(Richard Nixon)

As the last few days of the semester came to a close, students were reminded of several things. First, they had to be out of their dorms no later than Saturday, May 17. Similarly, students were reminded that graduation will take place in the Quadrangle on Saturday, May 17, beginning at 2:00pm. Most importantly, all students were reminded if they had borrowed silverware or glassware to please return the items to Rogers and Krise cafeteria ASAP.

Although the semester may be coming to a close for most students, the baseball team still had games to play, beginning with a weekend doubleheader against West Virginia Tech.

Founded in the latter years of the 19th century, the Montgomery Preparatory School for West Virginia University, as it was initially called, would undergo no less than four name changes in the half-century that followed. It wasn't until the early 1940's that the school would settle on the name it's known as today: the West Virginia Institute of Technology...WV Tech, for short. Located approximately one-third of the way between Charleston and Beckley, and a short distance off I-64/I-77, the school lies within the city of Montgomery. The town is named for James Montgomery, who first settled the land after it was given to him by his father-in-law as a wedding gift. The one-way distance from the Tech campus in the southern part of the state to the West Liberty campus in the northern part is nearly 220-miles and a full, three-and-half hour drive. This makes the trip one of the longest in the WL baseball schedule. With a student

135

enrollment of over 2,300, Tech is the fourth largest in the WVIAC, just behind WL's approximately 2,500 students. While the school is noted as a top-notch engineering school, it counts former NBA player, Sedale Threatt, as one of its more acclaimed alumni.

Saturday, May 3 vs. West Virginia Tech
(Overall 14-11, Conference 13-3)

The temperature was a warm 68 degrees when the first pitch crossed the plate at 1:00pm. In itself, this was a welcome sign since the temperature five-hours earlier was a "frosty" 49 degrees. The game-day conditions also included cloudy skies and steady winds from the South and East with gusts between 15 – 17mph.

In a lengthy, 10-paragraph article appearing in *The Trumpet* on Friday, May 9, entitled "Watson's Nine Takes Fourth Straight Win," the campus newspaper reports the game by sharing…

West Liberty's baseball team scored a
doubleheader victory over invading West
Virginia Tech, Saturday, May 3, to clinch a
fourth straight West Virginia Intercollegiate
Athletic Conference Northern Division crown.
The win earned the Hilltoppers the right to
meet Southern Division champ West Virginia
State in a best of three series Saturday and
Sunday, May 10-11, for the overall conference
crown. Senior captain Jon Kertes and freshman
Mark Stacy paced the Hilltoppers in a 13-6 win
in the opener. Both Kertes and Stacy rapped out
two singles and knocked in a run, while
designated hitter Gary West blasted a two-run
single. The Hilltoppers amassed 13 runs on
only several hits as Tech pitcher Jerry Williams
walked 10 batters to aid the Hilltopper cause.

*Dave Williams, who fanned nine batters, Picked
up the win. Bill Smiles and Dale Holstine had
two singles each for the losers. Gary
Freshwater tossed a five-hitter, whiffing seven,
to up his season record to 6-1 as the Hilltoppers
scored a 10-2 win in the nightcap. Coach Jim
Watson's club erupted for 11-hits as the hard-
hitting Kertes smashed a two-run homer in the
second inning and added a two-run single later
in the game. Rich Frey and Greg (sic) DeSantis
rapped two bingles each for WL. Gary Steck
belted a two-run double to account for Tech's
only tallies. WL is now 15-3 in the WVIAC play
and 16-10 overall.*

With the regular season, conference play now complete,
the Hilltoppers prepare for the last games of the '75 season,
two, seven-innings games, against the Bobcats of Frostburg
State College.

Founded in the waning years of the 1890s as a teacher's
college, Frostburg State is located in the city of Frostburg
(MD). The public college has a student enrollment of just
over 3,100, and the drive from the FSC campus to the WL
campus is a straight, 120-mile, 120-minute trip west on I-70.
The campus newspaper goes by the title of the Bottom Line.
Alumni of the school include Debra Monk, who won an
Academy Award in 1999 for playing the wife of Frank
Sipowitz in the award-winning series *NYPD Blue*, and
former MLB baseball coach, Jim Riggleman. Nicknamed the
Bobcats, and a mascot named Bob Cat, the '74 team
appeared in the NAIA District 18 playoffs and ended with a
25-12 record. Posting an 18-11 record coming into the game
with the Hilltoppers, the Bobcats are coached by Bob Wells,
who is in his 11th year as head coach.

Dr. Michael F. Price

Wednesday, May 7 vs. Frostburg State College
(Overall 16-11, Conference 15-3)
Another cold morning greeted the Hilltoppers for the game against FSC. The 8:00am temperature was an unfriendly 43 degrees. Still, by game time, the temperature had risen eighteen degrees to a manageable 61 degrees. With swirling winds that seemed to change by the minute, first from the ENE, changing to West, then to the WNW, and finally, from the North, the temperature at games' end had risen an incredible one degree!

With a headline "After Splitting Twinbill" and a subtitle "Hilltoppers Await Playoffs," the *Wheeling News-Register* of May 8 goes on to say...

After completing regular season action
yesterday by splitting a doubleheader with
Frostburg State on the home diamond West
Liberty State is now making final preparations
for this weekend's West Virginia Intercollegiate
Conference baseball playoff with West Virginia
State in Charleston...Yesterday's split gave the
'Toppers and 18-11 record, while State is just
12-19 overall but the Yellow Jackets captured
the Southern Division crown with a 11-9
conference mark. No other Southern Division
team in the Mountain State loop managed to
finish the campaign with a .500 mark. Left-
hander Ray Searage picked up the victory for
West Liberty in yesterday's opener, going all
the way for a 5-4 nod, scattering three hits but
walking six batters. A two-run double by
Calgelia in the seventh inning cut Hilltopper
victory margin to a single run. Jon Kertes
stroked a two-run triple and Jim Mellinger
homered and singled to pace the nine-hit West

Liberty attack. In the second game, Frostburg gained a 5-1 decision as O'Reilly tossed a seven-hitter. Mellinger had two of the 'Topper hits giving him a total of four on the day.

With a headline of "Bobcats Remain in Playoff Contention," an article in the May 8 edition of the *Cumberland Evening Times* records the game this way…

…The Bobcats split a twinbill at West Liberty College yesterday, coming back to win the nightcap 5-1 after dropping the opener 5-4. Frostburg was taking an 18-11 record into today's doubleheader and couldn't afford any setbacks in its bid for the postseason playoff berth. West Liberty jumped out to an early 3-0 in the first two innings against loser Bill Hunt in the opener on a two-out two run triple by Jon Kertes in the first and a solo homer by Jim Mellinger in the second. The Bobcats closed the gap to 3-2 in the third on a two-run double by John Calgelia but the Hilltoppers took advantage of two errors, an infield single and a walk to push across two more in the bottom of the third. Frostburg scored its final two runs in the seventh and had the tying run on second when the game ended. In the nightcap, former Bruce High standout Rick O'Reilly hurled a seven-hitter and Al Poklemba pounded a solo homer. Poklemba's homer broke a scoreless tie in the fourth inning and after the Vulvcans (sic) tied the score in the fifth O'Reilly sent in Rick Raughley with a squeeze bunt for the winning tally. The Bobcats added three more in the seventh with Shawn Baker and Raughley

rapping doubles.

Frostburg 4 W. Liberty 5
(First Game)

| Frostburg | 4 runs | 4 hits | 1 error |
| West Liberty | 5 runs | 9 hits | 0 errors |

Hunt and Bridgett; Serage (sic) and DeSantis

W. Liberty 1 Frostburg 5
(Second Game)

| Frostburg | 5 runs | 7 hits | 0 errors |
| West Liberty | 1 run | 7 hits | 1 error |

*O'Reilly and Calgelia, Bridgett; Bonar and DeSantis.
HR-Poklemba (Frostburg)*

Frostburg, a member of the Mason-Dixon Conference, would lose the final two games of their conference schedule and not make the district playoffs. The team would end the year with a 22-13 record.

––––––––––

With the regular season now complete and the postseason on the horizon, a quick review of the past two months' regular-season games is in order.

Of the 34-game schedule proposed at the beginning of the season, the Hilltoppers end-up playing in twenty-nine...the lone game with Columbus College (GA) on the southern trip, the conference doubleheader with Concord, and the non-conference twin-bill with the College of Steubenville...all rained out. The twenty-nine remaining games included eleven against non-conference teams and eighteen versus conference opponents. While the 'Toppers would finish with a 2-9 record against the likes of such powerhouse programs as UNC-W, Valdosta State College, and Marietta College, those eleven, non-conference teams would end the '75 season winning no less than a combined 200 games while losing around one hundred-twenty…a .625 winning percentage. In addition, three of the eleven teams would enter postseason play. The Blazers of Valdosta State would be one of four teams to play in the Division II South Atlantic Regionals in Lakeland, Florida. At the same time, UNC-W would appear in the NAIA College World Series tournament. Marietta College would finish runner-up in the 1975 NCAA Division II College World Series.

Of the seventeen opponents the Hilltoppers faced during the season, eight were non-conference schools, and nine were members of the WVIAC. Five of the non-conference schools had a larger student body, with West Virginia University's student enrollment being nearly seven-times larger than West Liberty's student population. With a student body about two-thirds of West Liberty, the smallest non-conference school that the 'Toppers played was Marietta College. The largest conference school played during the '75 season was Fairmont, while Davis and Elkins had the smallest student enrollment of WVIAC schools…less than 800.

If one considers the miles logged on the southern trip, while adding the travel to Concord College and Marietta College (OH), the odometer on the school van(s) would indicate that the team traveled nearly 2,900 miles during March…an average of about 100-miles a day! The four away games during April with WVIAC rivals Morris Harvey College (Charleston), Glenville State College (Glenville), West Virginia State (Institute), and Alderson Broaddus-College (Philippi), along with a non-conference doubleheader at California State College (PA), would total nearly 1,650 miles. In broad terms, the team traveled no less than 4,500 miles during the regular season.

The range of temperatures and weather conditions the team played in during the regular season conveyed a similar story of disparity. Average temperatures for the games with

Dr. Michael F. Price

UNC-W (NC), Jacksonville University, Florida A&M (FL), and Valdosta State College (GA) was 73 degrees. This range includes the 56 degrees, 1:00pm temperature for the UNC-W Seahawks game on March 8, and the 84-degree temperature for the game with the Blazers of VSC. The average for the scheduled March games against Concord and Marietta was 45 degrees. During the month, home and away games, the average temperature was an "unfriendly" 45 degrees. Far and away, the most unpleasant was the game with the Yellow Jackets of WV State, where the temperature at first pitch was 44 degrees. When the game ended nearly five hours later, the temperature had risen only 4 degrees! Although there was one day during the month of April when the game-time temperature was in the low 70's...the game versus Morris Harvey in Charleston...temperatures during the nine games that were played between April 2 and April 22 averaged an "encouraging" 54 degrees. The 'Toppers played under cloudy, mostly cloudy, or fair skies, and with varying degrees of wind.

Finally, it must be noted that between the opening game on March 8, and the last regular-season game with Frostburg State, May 7, the team played approximately 330-innings of baseball. The Hilltoppers played in two extra-inning games...both on the southern trip. Amid the 29-games, the 'Toppers scored no less than 149 runs while allowing around one-hundred one. In terms of scoring, the most lopsided loss came against Jacksonville University (9-3). At the same time, the most runs scored was the 'Toppers 15-1 victory against Glenville State. The WL team was shut-out twice during the season, once at the hands of Salem College (5-0) and the other versus the Vulcans of California State (3-0). Despite losing two doubleheaders (WVU and CSC), the opponents outscored 'Toppers during the four-games by only 8-runs (29 runs while WL scored 21). In sweeping six doubleheaders, the Hilltopper pitchers did not allow a single

142

run in four of the games…14-innings of scoreless ball versus Morris Harvey and seven innings each against Glenville and West Virginia Wesleyan. In those four shutout games, the 'Toppers outscored opponents 69-19. Lastly, the records show that the 'Toppers lost five one-run games, all against non-conference foes (UNC-W, Valdosta State, Marietta, WVU, and Frostburg).

The Hilltoppers would end the '75 regular season 17-12 overall while taking a 15-3 conference record into the three-game, winner takes all, WVIAC championship series against the Yellow Jackets of West Virginia State, May 10-11, at Watt Powell Park, in Charleston.

Built not long after World War II, Watt Powell Park has been the home of several minor league teams. The Charleston Senators, both a Single-A and later, a AAA farm team of the Washington Senators, was the first professional baseball team to call the stadium their home field. When the Senators relocated following the 1960 season, the stadium became the home to the Charleston Marlins of the International League, then the Charleston Indians, a AA affiliate of the Cleveland Indians, and currently, the Charleston Charlies, the AAA farm team of the Pittsburgh Pirates, who have been there since 1971. It is widely believed that Pirate farmhand, Dave Parker, hit the longest home run at Watt Powell Park during his tenure with the club in the early 1970s. Legend has it that Parker hit a ball out of the park, and it landed in a passing coal train. The ball was discovered as the coal was being unloaded in Columbus, OH. Because the park is the annual site of the WVIAC baseball championship games, it is familiar to several members of the current Hilltopper team, including seniors Dave Williams, Jon Kertes, and Robbie Schmidt, who has played in the winner-takes-all series for the past two years.

Moreover, this will be the Hilltoppers' second trip to Watt Powell Park this season. The team played Morris Harvey College at the park on April 2. This will be West Virginia State's first appearance at Watt Powell Park as a team in the championship series. On April 16, the Yellow Jackets hosted the Hilltoppers as the two teams split a doubleheader in Institute. The 'Toppers lost the first game 5-2 but won the second game 3-1. During the 2-day tournament, the team would stay at Morris Harvey College.

In a lengthy article authored by sportswriter Chuck Landon that appears in the May 8 edition of the *Charleston Daily News* and entitled "Young Yellow Jackets Surprise Coach By Reaching WVC Playoffs," WV State coach Bob Maxwell shares his feelings about the series with the 'Toppers.

...We're very excited about being in the playoffs
...We're looking forward to it. We feel it will be
a tremendous boost for the program. It should
help our recruiting...it should help everywhere.
When you get right down to it, it's what you
work for. It's what the game is all about. This
is the first time we've ever been in the playoffs
and I know it's been my goal for the five years
I've been here...We looked at this year as a
rebuilding season. I mean, there have been
other years when I thought we had far better
shots at it. This year everything seemed to fall
into place.

The schedule has the 'Toppers and the Yellow Jackets playing two games on Saturday, May 10, with a 1:00pm start. If needed, a third game will be played on Sunday, May 11, with the winner of the series advancing to the NAIA Area 7 playoffs. State comes into the series with a 12-19 record overall and finished first in the Southern Division. In contrast, WL comes in 17-12 overall and 15-3 in conference games. Going into the weekend series, Mike Lewis is hitting over .360 for WV State, while teammate, Jackie Hendricks, leads the team in home runs, rbi's, and stolen bases. Pitchers Eddie Ashbury and McCoy are a combined 8-4 record, and the pitching staff is allowing just over 4-runs a game.

Saturday, May 10 vs. WV State
(Overall 17-12, Conference 15-3)

The temperature was in the low-60s when the first pitch crossed the plate, marking the start of the game that would decide the WVIAC champs. There had been some rain in the area during the previous 24-hours, but the mostly cloudy skies at game time eventually gave way to fair skies. The winds from the South and West seemed to help the temperature to rise quickly to the middle-70's by 2:00pm.

(First Game)

The Hilltoppers would win the first game of the series by a score of 9-1. *The Tribune* (Coshocton, OH) issue of Sunday, May 11, with a byline of "Win In Playoffs," would forward this about the game...

> *David Williams, former Coshocton High School athlete and now a senior pitcher for the West Liberty Hilltoppers Baseball team, pitched a three-hit win over West Virginia State in WVIAC Playoffs Saturday at Powell Park, in a 9-1 victory. West Liberty also has Steve Zaugg as a player on the team.*

Reporting the game in the May 11 edition of the *Charleston Gazette-Mail*, Paul Wallace writes...
> *...in the opener, Lufft led the way with three hits in five tries and Jon Kertes and Shawn Girty*

145

drove in two runs each...

In addition to Lufft's three hits, Mark Stacy collected two hits and an RBI, Rich Frey also had two hits, while DeSantis, Duplaga, Kertes, Schmidt, and West each had one hit in the 12-hit, 9 run attack. In the run department, Schmidt and Lufft scored twice, DeMeo, DeSantis Kertes, Mellinger, and West contributed in the 'Toppers nine runs. WLSC hitters were 12-38 for a .316 average. The State batters were 4-32 for a .125 average. While the 'Toppers would commit 2 errors (Lufft, Frey), the Yellow Jackets would commit 6 errors...five by the State third baseman. The Hilltoppers left 12 runners on base, and the Yellow Jackets left seven.

West Liberty	*9 runs*	*13 hits*	*2 errors*
WV State	*1 run*	*4 hits*	*6 errors*

Williams (WP)	*4H, 1R, 1BB, 11SO*
McCoy (LP)	*6H, 3R, 3BB, 3SO*
Carter	*3H, 5R, 3BB, 0SO*
Warner	*3H, 1R*
Magnemi	

Saturday, May 10 vs. WV State
(Second Game)
(Overall 18-12, Conference 15-3)
With a bold headline in all caps that read "SPLIT, State Rallies to Force Third Playoff Game," Paul Wallace in the May 11, *Charleston Gazette-Mail*, writes...
West Virginia State scored three runs in the
top of the ninth inning to edge West Liberty,
8-5, Saturday in the second game of a
doubleheader and forced a third game to be
played at 2:00 p.m. today at Watt Powell Park
for the West Virginia Conference championship.

...After the Hilltoppers rallied to tie the nightcap with three runs in the eighth, Mike Lewis smacked a two-run triple to drive in the deciding runs for the Yellow Jackets in the ninth. Ron Carter opened the ninth with a walk and was sacrificed to second. Bruce Knell, who earlier hit a two-run home run over the left field fence, was intentionally walked. Lewis then tripled down the left field line. Jackie Hendricks followed with a double to right center to score Lewis. West Liberty loaded the bases with one out in the bottom half of the ninth with two singles and an error. Freshman Joe Magnemi, who picked up the win in relief, struck out Tom Lufft and got Stan Duplaga to ground out to Curt Waldron at second to end the game.

While each team had ten hits in the game, Kertes led the Hilltoppers with three hits, DeSantis and Schmidt each had two, and Girty, Frey, and Stacy one hit each. WLSC hitters were 10-42 for a .238 average. The State batters were 12-36 for a .333 average. The 'Toppers would again leave a dozen men on base to seven for State.

WV State	*8 runs*	*10 hits*	*4 errors*
West Liberty	*5 runs*	*10 hits*	*1 error*

Asbury	*8H, 4R, 2BB, 9SO*
Magnemi (WP)	*2H, 1R, 2SO*
Freshwater (LP)	*10H, 8R, 3BB, 10SO*

With both possessing a victory in the short, 3-game series, the teams left Watt Powell Park with the decisive game set for the next day and a 1:00pm start.

147

Sunday, May 11 vs. WV State
(Third Game)
(Overall 18-13, Conference 15-3)

As the Hilltopper squad left the confines of their hotel mid-morning, they were met with temperatures in the mid-to-high '50s, partly cloudy skies, and a slight breeze from the South and West. By game time, the temperature had reached a comfortable 73 degrees. In a short time, the Yellow Jackets of WV State would face a storm brought on by Hilltopper hitting and pitching.

"W. Liberty Baseballers In Survival Tilt Today" read the headline on May 12…

…The two teams split in a doubleheader on Saturday, with the Hilltoppers winning the front game, 9-1, and State picking up the win in the nightcap, 8-5. Dave Williams tossed a four-hitter in the opener, striking out 11 batters, as the Hilltopper bats erupted for 13 hits. Senior captain Jon Kertes led the way with a two-run double while Shawn ,9irty (sic) knocked in two runs and Mark Stacy rapped a double and a single. Tom Lufft, former Wheeling High star, belted three bingles and Rick Frye (sic) had two hits for the 'Toppers. Mike Lewis had two singles for State. Both teams had 12 hits in the second contest but State got three tallies in the final inning to pull out the victory and keep its title hopes alive. Bruce Knell smacked a two-run homer while Lewis connected for a triple and a single, knocking in three runs, and Rick Walker had a double and a single for State. Kertes once again led the Black and Gold charges with a

*double, two singles and two RBI's while Girty,
Robbie Schmidt, and Greg (sic) DeSantis had
two singles each. Coach Jim Watson with (sic)
send freshman, Ray Searage, from Deer
Park, NY, against State's Charlie McKinney
in today's championship contest. The winner
receives the District 28 berth in the NAIA Area 7
championships slated for later this month. If
the Hilltoppers win today, the event will likely
be played at the West Liberty diamond.* *

In an article that ran in the *Weirton Daily Times* on
Monday, May 12, entitled "Hilltoppers Again Reign Over
WVIAC," the paper had this to say about the third and
deciding game of the series...

*West Liberty erupted for a five-run first inning
Sunday and choked off W. Va. State's rallies to
clobber the Yellow Jackets, 13-5, handing the
Hilltoppers their third straight West Virginia
Conference baseball crown. Robby (sic)
Schmidt, Jon Kertes, and Jim Mellinger cracked
three straight doubles in the Hilltoppers' first
inning bonanza. State trimmed West Liberty's
lead to 5-2 but the Hilltoppers' infield crew
pulled off three double plays to stop any scoring
threat the rest of the way...West Liberty starter
Ray Searage, who got all but the final out of the
game, fanned a dozen Yellow Jackets while
yielding five runs and nine walks. The year
ended for State on a 13-21 log. West Liberty,
finishing its WVC campaign with a 19-12 (sic)
mark, heads into the NAIA area playoffs at an
as yet an undetermined site.*

A similar article entitled "West Liberty Claims 3rd WVC Title in Row" appeared in *The Wheeling Intelligencer* on Monday, May 12, saying…

The third time proved a charm for West Liberty in more ways than one. The Hilltopper baseball team Sunday afternoon wrapped up its third straight West Virginia Conference title in the third game of its best-of-three WVC divisional playoff against W.Va. State. WLS struck early with five runs in the first inning at Wyatt Powell Park and overpowered the Yellow Jackets 13-5. WLS (20-1) (sic) now will represent District 28 in the NAIA Area 7 championships tentatively scheduled for May 20-23 at a West Virginia site to be determined. The Hilltoppers pulled out to a 13-2 upper hand behind the slants of Ray Searage until the ninth frame when frosh reliever Mark Fabbro, of Oak Glen Glen (sic), snuffed out a three-run rally with two strikeouts. In the key first inning for the Hilltoppers, Rob Schmidt doubled home Shawn Girty and Mark Stacy while Jon Kertes and Jim Mellinger collected doubles and Tom Lufft singled in a run. Greg (sic) DeSantis ended with three rbi's while Schmidt, Kertes, and Mellinger knocked in two each. Overall, the Hilltopper bats collected 13 hits and the victors didn't commit an error to back the six-hit pitching by Searage and Fabbro. W.Va. State wound up with a 13-21 record.

In an article entitled "Loss Doesn't Dull State's Rosy Future," the *Charleston Daily News* of Monday, May 12, writes that…

The loss did not dull State coach Bob

*Maxwell's optimum, however. "We have
basically a young team, so we hope to be back
for a few years," Maxwell said...West Liberty
now advances to the National Association of
Intercollegiate Athletics regional tournament
June 2-3 at a West Virginia site to be
determined. Rob Schmidt got West Liberty
started with a two-run double after singles by
Shawn Girty and Mark Stacy...Winning pitcher
Ray Searage, 5-2, allowed seven hits and
needed ninth-inning relief help from Mark
Fabbro to gain the decision. A two-run single
by Mike Lewis allowed State to close within
5-2 in the third. But the Hilltoppers put the
game away with six unearned runs in the sixth
and seventh innings. State committed four
errors in that two-inning stretch...*

On Monday, May 12, the *Morgantown Dominion Post*, in
an article entitled "West Liberty Grabs Crown," chronicles...
*"...They played excellent ball," State coach
Bob Maxwell said. "They hit the ball well and
had several double plays to kill us. We have
basically a young team, so we hope to be back
for a few years..."*

Opening with the title "For Third Straight Year," and a
subtitle that reads "Hilltoppers Open Fast, Down State for
Title," Staff Sports Writer, Paul Wallace, of the *Charleston
Gazette-Mail*, writes on May 12, that...
*...State scored three useless runs in the ninth
as relief pitcher Joe Magnemi singled in Joe
Wallace. Curt Waldron, playing for Jim
Charley, who was injured Saturday, then
doubled to score Kenny Williams and Randy*

Harpold singled to score Waldron…

| West Liberty | 13 runs | 10 hits | 0 errors |
| WV State | 5 runs | 7 hits | 4 errors |

E-Carter, Marion, Hendricks, Warner, LOB – WL 8, State 9, 2b – Schmidt, Kertes, Mellinger, Waldron; DP – WL 3; S – DeSantis, West; SB Harpold

Searage (WP)	*6H, 5R, 9BB, 12SO*
Fabbro	*2SO*
McKinney (LP)	*6H, 7R, 4BB, 3SO*
Carter	*1H, 1R, 1BB*
Warner	*3H, 5R, 2BB*
Magnemi	*2SO*

Robbie Schmidt, Jon Kertes, and Jim Mellinger each had a double in the win. Also collecting hits in the 'Topper, 10-hit Sunday slugfest, were Gregg DeSantis, Stan Duplaga, Tom "T" Lufft, Robbie Schmidt, Mark Stacy, and Gary "Harley" West. Schmidt, Kertes, Mellinger (Melby), and DeSantis each had two rbi's, while Shawn Girty scored three times. As a team, the Hilltoppers went 10 for 36…a .278 clip. Conversely, WV State batters ended up 7 for 29…a .241 average…with State stars Mike Lewis and Jackie Hendricks going a combined 1 for 7 in the deciding game. Yellow Jacket coach Maxwell used a total of 18 players, including four pitchers. West Liberty used 12 players and two pitchers. West Virginia State ends the season with a record of 13-21. At the same time, the Hilltoppers not only upped their overall record to 19-13 but also extended the season.

With a byline of "West Liberty In NAIA Field," the article in the *Wheeling News-Register* of May 12 leads…
On a day when West Liberty State's baseball

152

team scored 13 runs and pounded out 13 hits to retain its West Virginia Intercollegiate Conference championship for the third year, Coach Jim Watson preferred to talk about pitching and defense. "Ray Searage did a great job on the mound and our infield turned over three double players which wiped out any chance they had of coming back," commented the enthusiastic Watson after the Hilltoppers 13-5 rout of West Virginia State in the deciding game of the best-of-three series, which ends the winner on to the national competition via a berth in the NAIA Area 7 eliminations. Searage, a freshman lefty from Long Island, struck out 12 and gave up just six hits before tiring in the ninth when another plebe Mark Fabbro came on to get the last out with still another strikeout. West Liberty played errorless ball as Searage gained his fifth win in seven decisions and raised the Gold and Black's overall record to 20-12 (sic). A five-run outburst in the top of the first broke it open early. "We were ready and came right at them," said the still beaming Watson. Back-to-back singles by Shawn Girty and Mark Stacy started the uprising. After a sacrifice bunt by DeSantis, Robbie Schmidt followed with a two-rundouble to make it 2-0 while Jon Kertes doubled and Jim Mellinger singled for two more runs. The final tally scored when Tom Lufft's single eluded the centerfielder for a two-base error. West Liberty scored another run in the fifth and Girty's two-run single highlighted a three-run splurge in the sixth frame. The Hilltoppers then got four runs in the seventh, the (sic) with Lufft and Stacy

153

both collecting two-run singles.

With a headline the reads "Mellinger, Kertes lead WLSC to crown," the article goes on to say…

Jim Mellinger and Jon Kertes, two Jewett outfielders, were instrumental last week in leading West Liberty State College to its third consecutive West Virginia Conference baseball championship and an NAIA play-off spot. Kertes, a senior and team captain, had a two-run double in the first contest and drove in two more in the nightcap with a double and two singles. Mellinger, is a junior, and joins Kertes in batting well over .300 for the season. Also a member of the championship team is Adena's Ed Dulkoski, a relief pitcher … *

Jim Mellinger, Jon Kertes

*Conference Trophy: left to right, Jon Kertes, Coach Watson,
Rob Schmidt, Dave Williams*

Without a doubt, the win against the Yellow Jackets earlier that day made the nearly 200-mile, three-hour trip from Charleston to West Liberty an enjoyable one. However, the players and staff had little time to celebrate because the next week would be a busy one. First, Monday, May 12, would begin five-days of final exams for most students. While the test schedule would play havoc with Hilltopper practices, the players knew that this was a time when academics was paramount over athletics. The busy week would conclude with graduation taking place for all seniors, including two team members, Dave Williams and Jon Kertes.

It was most likely during the week of exams that Coach Watson received word that the next stop for the team will be NAIA, Area 7 playoffs, in Greensboro, NC. The four-team, double-elimination tournament is scheduled to begin on Thursday, May 22, with the championship game set for Saturday afternoon, May 24. Along with the 'Toppers, the recently crowned champions of District 28, the participating teams will include District 6 winner, the Indians of Newberry College (SC), High Point College (NC) Panthers from District 26, and a familiar face from earlier in the year, the UNC-W Seahawks (NC), representing District 29. The opening game of the tournament on Thursday, May 22, will

155

pit Newberry against West Liberty at 6:30pm, while the nightcap will see host High Point College taking on UNC-W. Friday afternoon's game will see the losers of Game 1 and 2 facing off, with the losing team being eliminated. Following Game 3, the winners of Thursday's games will go head-to-head in Game 4. The loser of Game 4 will then play the winner of Game 3, with the loser sent packing. The Area 7 championship game will be held on Saturday, May 24, with the winning team moving on to participate in the NAIA College World Series in St. Joseph, MO.

In a series of pre-tourney articles, the *Weirton Daily Times* of May 17 records that...

Gregg DeSantis, an ex-Madonna ballplayer
and Gary Freshwater, and Gary Freshwater, a
Brooke product, are members of the WVIAC
champion West Liberty State College squad,
which will start NAIA Regional play next week
in North Carolina...

Following a headline that read "Hilltopper Tourney Game on Thursday," an article in the May 20 edition of the *Wheeling News-Register*, states...

The West Liberty State baseball team left for
Greensboro, N.C., but won't get to play until
Thursday night when the Hilltoppers take on
Newberry (SC) College in the opening game of
the NAIA Area 7 playoffs. The double
elimination tournament was originally set to
get underway Wednesday night but host High
Point (N.C.) College was plagued by rain
in its district playoffs...

The Season That Was

Paul Shinn, Associate Sports Editor, writing in a lead-up article in the May 21 edition of the *High Point Enterprise*, shares that…

The High Point College baseball team has been involved in four Area 7 tournaments, but this year is the first that the Panthers are acting as host institution for the four-team, double-elimination event. The teams will be housed at High Point College, but games have been scheduled for Greensboro Memorial Stadium because the field at HPC has no lights. The revised schedule for the weekend of play is this: The tournament will open Thursday evening at 6 with Newberry playing West Liberty State, followed by an 8:30 game with High Point taking on UNC-Wilmington. Losers play Friday at 2, followed by night games at 6 and 8:30. In a departure from the last two tournaments HPC was in, the finals of the area will be held Saturday afternoon at 2 and 4 instead of Saturday night…Only one team came in early, West Liberty had a long drive from West Virginia and arrived Monday night to rest up. The other two are expected today. Originally, West Virginia was to have hosted the tournament, but it was moved here after complications.

In a May 21 article entitled "West Liberty Tourney Bid Set Thursday," the *Steubenville Herald-Star* forwards that…
Coach Jim Watson's Hilltoppers, appearing in their third straight NAIA playoff series, go against Newberry, SC, in the 6:30pm tourney lidlifter. The team departed West Liberty Monday and arrived in Greensboro Tuesday

*night for the double-elimination event. The
Hilltoppers, winners of the West Virginia
Conference and the NAIA District 28, boast
several players from the Steubenville area.
They are Mark Stacy, Big Red, second
baseman; Rick Spencer, Big Red, reserve
catcher; Ed Dulkoski, Cadiz, pitcher; Gary
Freshwater, Colliers, pitcher; Mark Fabbro,
Newell pitcher; Jim Mellinger, Jewett,
outfielder; Jon Kertes, Germano, outfielder;
and Greg (sic) DeSantis, Follansbee, catcher.
Steubenville's Stacy is the team's second leading
hitter with a .325 average. Jewett's Mellinger is
third at .321 while Kertes is batting at .290.
DeSantis is hitting at a .283 clip. The leader is
Jim (sic) Schmidt of Wheeling at .356.
Freshwater, former Brooke High mound star,
takes a 6-2 record into the tourney. The 6'3",
210-pound righthander, has a 2.60 earned run
average. The best on the team. He has logged
54 strikeouts. Fabro (sic), former Oak Glen
star, has a 1-2 record but has recorded 2 saves.
Dulkoski is 0-2 but has one save to his credit...*

In the following day's edition of the *High Point
Enterprise*, Shinn adds in a lengthy article...
*...Newberry and West Liberty have both been
idle for 11 days following their district playoffs.
Wilmington has had five days off...High Point
will be favored (against UNC-W) because of its
40-4 record but...Wilmington is the team for the
Panthers to beat...Pairings are made on a
rotation, so that each district opens against a
different district every year. High Point got to
choose its starting time because it is host*

school. Wilmington has a 24-9-1 record..."We
have three freshmen in our starting pitching
rotation and I wouldn't want to say who was
number one," Brooks (UNC-W head coach)
said. "I will tell you we aren't going to let Otis
Foster hit against us like he's been doing all
year. We'll walk him a lot"...Foster has 29
home runs and is hitting around .500. He hit
three homers in the final district game. On top
of that, he strikes out infrequently for a slugger.
Behind Foster is Danny Goins, who has upped
his homer total to 13...The West Liberty State
Hilltoppers come from way up in the mountains.
At one time they were to have hosted the
tournament, but couldn't get enough sponsor
money to make it worthwhile. Coach James
Watson is in his fourth year at the school.
West Liberty has an enrollment of 3,000.
Gary Freshwater is the top pitcher with a
6-3 record. Infielder Rob Schmidt is the
leading hitter with a .356 average. The
Hilltoppers have two other .300 hitters in
Jim Mellinger and Mark Stacy.*

In a headline *"Newberry Opposes West Liberty St.,"* the
Greenville News (Greenville, SC) ran an article in the May
22 edition and saw things this way...

*Newberry opens the NAIA Region Seven
baseball tournament at Greensboro (N.C.)
War Memorial Stadium Thursday night,
when the Indians take on West Liberty State
College (W.Va.) at 6:00pm. Coach Horace
Turbeville will start ace right-hander Roland
Thomas. Thomas compiled a 5-2 won-loss
record over the season, and a 1.33 earned run*

average, both tops on Newberry's pitching staff. Turbeville considers his team to be about the equal of West Liberty State. Most observers of the tournament predict, however, that the two North Carolina teams in the tournament, High Point and UNC-Wilmington, should be rated the favorites...

In a May 22 article in the *Wheeling News-Register* headlined "NAIA Tourney At Greensboro: West Liberty vs. Newberry," Nick Bedway, Associate Sports Editor, writes...

West Liberty carries a 19-13 record into its third straight NAIA tourney appearance. The Hilltoppers have compiled an impressive record in the four years Jim Watson has been their head coach, winning the Northern Division title in the West Virginia Intercollegiate Conference all four years and capturing the loop playoffs the last three years. Under Watson's direction, the Gold and Black baseballers have an overall won-lost record of 70-38, including a sparkling 56-16 conference mark. Highly pleased to be back in the national eliminations, Watson feels the Hilltoppers have a legitimate chance for a good showing. "We're stronger defensively and we have much more pitching depth than we had last year," he insisted, despite the fact that the West Virginians start three new faces in the infield. "We turned over 17 double plays and our team batting average is 90 points higher than our opponents." A hard-luck victim on several occasions, Williams has compiled a 4-4 record along with a 2.75 ERA in 72 innings of work. After Williams, the Hilltopper coach will turn to

*junior Gary Freshwater in the Friday game.
Freshwater has a 6-2 record with a 2.60 ERA in
55 13 (sic) innings. Should WLSC stay alive in
the tournament, freshman lefty Ray Searage, the
winning hurler in the WVIC championship game
against West Virginia State, will get the nod.
Three West Liberty regulars batting above the
.330 level are Robbie Schmidt with a .356
average, Mark Stacy hitting at a .325 clip, and
Jim Mellinger hitting at a .321 clip. Last year's
top batsman, Jon Kertes, has a .290 average, but
he's been climbing in recent weeks and leads the
team in RBI's with 29. Schmidt has clouted a
team high eight homers and has 28 ribbies...*

And finally, Rod Hackney, Sports Staff Writer with the *Greensboro Daily News*, writes in the May 22 edition of the newspaper…

*...High Point, which captures the District 26
title Monday by defeating Pfeiffer, is considered
the favorite. The Panthers have compiled a 40-4
record...Otis Foster, who leads the nation's
small colleges in home runs and RBI's, tops
the High Point offensive attack. The slugging
Panther senior owns an amazing .493 batting
average and 76 runs and 29 home runs.
Danny Goins is another High Point standout.
The senior leftfielder is hitting at a .329 clip
and has 13 home runs to his credit. The
Panther pitching is led by Dan England...
England has lost only one game in 13 starts
and owns a 1.84 ERA. He also has 105
strikeouts. UNC-Wilmington defeated
Methodist College in the District 29
tournament in order to advance to the Area 7*

*playoffs. The Seahawks, who own a 24-9
record are led in hitting by senior Robert
Pittman with a .326 batting average and 29
RBIs...Newberry represents District 7 with a
16-7 season mark. The Indians bested Baptist
College for a berth here. Senior Don Moore
heads the list of Newberry slugging threats
with a .395 batting average...(High Point
Coach) Hartman tabbed West Liberty as the
underdog in this week's tournament which had
originally been planned for West Virginia, but
was moved when sufficient sponsorship could
not be raised. "They have not done well here
in the past," the Panther coach said. "In
fact, I don't think they've even won more than
one game in this tournament before."*

Founded in 1856, Newberry College, a private school affiliated with ELCA (Lutheran), is located in Newberry, SC, in the west-central part of the state. During the Civil War, the college was used as a hospital for Confederate troops. With a student enrollment of less than 900, Newberry College would be the second smallest school the Hilltoppers would play in '75...only Davis and Elkins has fewer students. Among the Newberry alumni is Lee Atwater, advisor to Presidents Reagan and George H.W. Bush. The Indians are coached by Horace Turbeville, who is in his 8th year.

Thursday, May 22 vs. Newberry
(Overall 19-13, Conference 15-3)

Upon leaving the dorms at High Point College and traveling North on I-85, the team arrived at War Memorial Stadium after a 30-minute ride. As anticipated, the weather conditions were typical for central North Carolina in late May. The temperature at game time was an uncomfortable 89 degrees, humidity in the mid-50s, light winds from the SSW, with fair/mostly cloudy skies. Newspapers from four states…North Carolina, Ohio, Pennsylvania, and South Carolina, carried the game results.

With a byline of "High Point Belted in Area 7 Action," the *Burlington (NC) Daily Times-News* records on May 23 that…

*West Liberty State scored eight runs in the sixth
inning on its way to a 10-5 victory over
Newberry in Thursday night opening game of
the NAIA Area 7 baseball tournament…West
Liberty had taken a one-run lead in the bottom
of the second inning against Newbery when
rightfielder Jim Mellinger scored on a double
off the bat of third baseman Stan Duplaga.
Newberry came back with five hits in the top of
the fifth to score four runs. The Newberry
Indians were led in the big inning by the hitting
of first baseman Steve Robertson, who drove in
two runs with a double. But the roof fell in on
the Indians in the next inning.*

"Hilltops Dump Newberry," read the headline, and the story continued, saying…

*…West Liberty opened the sixth inning rally
when left fielder Jon Kertes scrambled to first
base one step ahead of the throw from
Newberry third baseman Charles Camp…
Kertes came home on a double by Mellinger
to wind up the Hilltopper scoring parade…
The Hilltoppers added another run in the
seventh to put the icing on the cake.
Newberry managed to squeeze in a final run
its last chance at bat, but it was too little
and much too late…*

On the same day, the *Steubenville Herald-Star* shares…

*…Against Newberry (16-8) yesterday, the West
Liberty team (20-13) trailed 4-1 before erupting
for eight runs in the home half of the sixth
inning. The stars of the game were Jon Kertes
and Jim Mellinger, Jewett-Scio products who
had went to bat twice and each time delivered
base hits. Kertes had a 3-run double after
singling and scoring the first run of the inning.
Freshman Stan Duplaga aided the cause via a
pair of singles as the Hilltoppers matched
Newberry's 12 hits. Rick Bonar, sophomore
from River Local, relieved starter Dave
Williams, who was tagged for a two-run double
by Steve Robertson to feature Newberry's 4-run
fifth, and held the losers to five hits the
remaining 4 and two-thirds innings. **

Noting "West Liberty Gains in NAIA," the *Pittsburgh
Post-Gazette* chronicles…

*West Liberty State College, behind the hitting
of Robby (sic) Schmidt and Shawn Girty,
thumped Newberry, S.C., 10-5, in the first
round of the NAIA Area 7 playoffs yesterday.
Schmidt hit two singles and drove in a run,
and Girty got three hits and drove in two runs
in the rout. West Liberty moves into the
second round of this double elimination
tournament today. The tourney winner goes
into the NAIA world series in St. Joseph, Mo.*

The *Greenville (SC) News* summed-up the game by
reporting that…

West Liberty sent 11 men to the plate in the

*sixth inning, scored eight runs and handed
Newberry a 10-5 defeat in the opening round of
the NAIA baseball tournament Thursday...West
Liberty team captain Jon Kertes led the
Hilltopper uprising with a double and a single
in the sixth. His double knocked in three runs
and he scored both times he reached base in the
inning. Stan Duplaga had two hits for West
Liberty and knocked in two runs. Newberry,
now 16-8, led 4-1 with a four-run fifth inning
off starter Dave Williams. But Rick Bonar
relieved Williams, stopped the Indians and
finished the game to pick up his fourth victory.**

With the title "West Liberty Cops Tournament Opener,"
the May 23 edition of the *Wheeling News-Register* says this
about the Newberry game...

*Easy winners in Thursday's first round games
here, West Liberty State and the University of
North Carolina-Wilmington Branch, play at
2 p.m. today in the NAIA baseball
championships...Wilmington won its initial
tourney test in a surprising fashion, routing
the High Pointers by a 14-5 score for its 25
victory in 34 games. The Hilltoppers,
meanwhile, got excellent relief pitching from
sophomore lefty Rick Bonar, who scattered
five hits and allowed just one run over the
last 4 2-3 innings, in downing Newberry 10-5,
for its 20th victory against 13 setbacks.
Coach Jim Watson's three-time West
Virginia Intercollegiate Conference champions
erased a 4-1 deficit by exploding for eight runs
in the bottom of the sixth inning. Twelve men
went to the plate in the uprising with Jon*

*Kertes and Jim Mellinger collecting two hits
and scoring twice each. Kertes tallied the first
run after banging out a single and later blasted
a three-run double for the crunching blow.
Other big batsmen for the winners included
Shawn Girty with three hits and Stan Duplaga
with a pair of doubles. Staring hurlers in this
afternoon's game were expected to be right-
hander Gary Freshwater, with a 6-2 record for
West Liberty, and Wilmington freshman Mike
Hunter. This will be the second meeting of the
year between the two clubs. Wilmington took a
4-3 decision in 10 innings over the Gold and
Black during West Liberty's annual spring
junket in March.*

Newberry	*5 runs*	*12 hits*	*4 errors*
West Liberty	*10 runs*	*12 hits*	*5 errors*

*Thomas, Crocker (6), Driggers (7), and Rowland;
Williams, Bonar (5), and DeFantis (sic); WP – Bonar,
LP –Thomas
Extra Base Hits: 2b-Robertson (N) 2, Privette (N), Hollis
(N), Duplaga (W) 2, Kertes (W)
A-2,000 (Est)*

"W. Liberty A Serious Contender," writes Paul Shinn, in
the *High Point Enterprise* edition of May 23.
*West Liberty State didn't come all this far to be
made sport of...Thursday, West Liberty ran by
Newberry 10-5 with an eight run sixth inning
that erased a 4-1 Newberry lead. "This is our
third trip to the area tournament," said WLS
coach Jim Watson. "The most we've won is one
game and we'd like to improve things from our*

previous start." West Liberty relies heavily on young ball players. It started three freshmen in the infield last night. One of those, Stan Duplaga, got two doubles, scored twice, and knocked in a run from his eighth spot in the lineup. His senior teammate Jon Kertes had a bases-loaded double in the big sixth to plate three. According to Watson it's a wonder he could do much. "The double gave us the big boost," Watson said, "but he has had an eye infection and can hardly see, especially in the field." "Actually we played poorly in most aspects but I can't complain with a win. Newberry was stronger than we thought, but I think we're stronger than a lot of people think. We had the momentum after the big inning, but I think Newberry is capable of coming back and winning in this tournament"...The home team sent 12 men to the plate in the sixth before Jerry Driggers could get the side out in relief. Hits were plentiful with Newberry getting 13 and West Liberty 11. Both sides made four errors. West Liberty got a break of sorts in the fourth when Newberry's Robertson double to right hit the top of the wall and bounced back into play. Had the bounce gone the other way, it would have been a home run. Robertson hit a double to right in the ninth and later scored, but by that time, West Liberty of District 28 had already put the pretty much out of reach.

In the late game, the Seahawks of UNC-W topped host team, High Point College, by a 14-5 score. The victors rapped out 16 hits, five by the third baseman and number eight hitter in the line-up, Bob Schupp, and three by the number nine hitter, Swain Smith.

With a byline of "Panthers Need to 'Mature,'" Paul Shinn writes in the *High Point Enterprise* of May 23 that...

*...(High Point Coach) Hartman had some time
to think about things. Not only did the game
run well over three hours, but Hartman spent
a lot of that time outside the playing field after
he had been thrown out in the top of the fifth
for arguing with the plate umpire. Supposedly,
the ump and (High Point) catcher Chuck Sharp
got into a debate over some calls and the ump
made the mistake of letting Hartman hear.
He zipped from the dugout, got in his piece
and got the thumb. "I had to protect my player,"
he said. "I was always taught that if you
didn't try to show the other guy up when
talking about calls, you weren't
supposed to get into this type of thing Sharp
and the ump were in. The ump said Sharp
crossed him, but I've had Sharp four years
and when he told me he didn't, I have to believe
him...After a while we got to playing the umps
instead of the other team. We paniced (sic)."
Two Wilmington pitchers walked 13 batters,
while three from HPC walked 10.*

With the loss to UNC-W, High Point College moves into the loser's bracket and is scheduled to play Newberry in the first game of the Friday session, which begins at 2:00pm. The night session will be a rematch of a game between West Liberty and UNC-W that took place on March 8 in Wilmington, which the Seahawks won 4-3 in 11 innings. The loser of the WL vs. UNC-W game will face host HPC on

Friday, with the loser of that game packing their bags and heading home.

Friday, May 23 vs. UNC-W
(Overall 20-13, Conference 15-3)

With a 6:00pm first pitch, the Hilltopper game versus UNC-W was the second game of the day. Thanks to a welcomed rain around 3:00pm, the temperature in the area fell nearly 20 degrees to a comfortable 69 degrees by game time. Just as in March, when the Hilltoppers lost by one-run to the Seahawks, UNC-W would once more prevail against 'Toppers. The score this time was 8-7. More disappointing, however, than another one-run loss could be the way the game ended.

In an article in the *High Point Enterprise* of May 24 with the headline "Strange Ending Favors UNC-W," Paul Shinn writes…

If West Liberty State is as 'down'…as it looked Friday night after losing 8-7 to UNC-Wilmington, the Hilltoppers may only go through the motions of playing in the loser's bracket of the Area 7 baseball tournament… Wilmington scored a single run in the last of the ninth to rally from an early 4-0 deficit to remain the only unbeaten team in the double elimination event. It appeared West Liberty was out of the inning with a tie when all of a sudden the Wilmington players started cheering, leaving most everybody else stunned. What really happened was the West Liberty catcher was charged with interference on the batter's swing that would have been the third out of the inning. Robert Ivey was awarded first base to score Van Lewis with the winner. The bases had been loaded after one out. West

Liberty reliever Ray Serage (sic) seemed to be working out of trouble when he got Howie Edgerton to pop to third. Then Ivey popped foul begin first. The teams were about to change sides when the call came. West Liberty coach Jim Watson protested briefly, but the decision stood. As ever, winning coach Bill Brooks didn't act surprised. "It was a strange way to end the ball game," he said. "But the umpire had to call it. Everybody heard the interference. It's a rule and it has to be called. The ump didn't have any other choice"... Wilmington scored four in the eighth on three hits, the big blow being Swain Smith's home run to center wins off reliever Mark Fabbro after hehad relieved starter Gary Freshwater. West Liberty scored three to open the game and lost some more after lead-off batter Shawn Girty had his double taken away on an appeal he missed first base. Later the Hilltoppers lost another chance when offensive interference was called on a batter for running into his fair ball. Those plays should have been a tip off of things to come.

| West Liberty | 7 runs | 12 hits | 6 errors |
| UNC-W | 8 runs | 10 hits | 0 errors |

Freshwater, Fabbro (8), Searage (9) and DeSantis Hunter, Watkins (1), Prosser and Ourt W – Prosser (5-10) L – Searage (5-2) HR – File, Smith

The *Steubenville Herald-Star* reported the game this way...

...West Liberty led for most of the game, but UNCW tied it at 7-7 with four hits in the eighth inning. In the bottom of the ninth, the bases loaded and two outs, the umpire ruled interference by catcher Gregg DeSantis, whose mit inadvertently got in the way of baller Robert Ivey's bat, causing him to pop up. The umpire sent Ivey to first base, walking in the winning run.*

Following a between game break, the Hilltoppers took the field to play against High Point College. The winner of the game would return the next day to play the Seahawks of UNC-W for the right to represent Area 7 in the NAIA College World Series, and the loser would be eliminated.

A private school founded in 1924 and affiliated with the United Methodist Church, High Point College has a student enrollment of just over 1,000, or about half the size of West Liberty. The school is surrounded by the city High Point, and with sister cities Greensboro and Winston-Salem, the city comprises one-third of the Piedmont Triad. Not only is the city known as the only North Carolina city that extends into four counties, but it is also recognized as the furniture capital of the world and the home of Thomas Buses (those yellow school buses that one sees every day). High Point College alumni include Donna Fargo (country music singer) and Tubby Smith (college basketball coach). After losing too UNC-W on Thursday, the Panthers enter Friday's game against the 'Toppers with a record of 40-5. The team is coached by Chuck Hartman, who is coaching in his 15th season.

*Friday, May 23 vs. High Point College
(Second Game)*

Dr. Michael F. Price

(Overall 20-14, Conference 15-3)
Playing for the second time in less than three hours, the Hilltoppers would fall to the host team by a score of 5-1. The *Burlington (NC) Daily-Times Daily* wrote this about the game...

> *First inning home runs by Otis Foster and*
> *Danny Goins put High Point on its way...to a*
> *5-1 victory over West Liberty State, eliminating*
> *the West Virginia club in the NAIA Area 7*
> *baseball tournament...High Point opened*
> *against West Liberty with two runs on Foster's*
> *30th homer of the year, and Goin's 14th of the*
> *year. In the bottom of the ninth, Tom Lufft*
> *doubled and came home on a fielder's choice*
> *from West Liberty's lone run.*

| High Point | 5 runs | 9 hits | 1 error |
| West Liberty | 1 runs | 10 hits | 1 error |

Idol and Sharp, Searage and DeSantis

The *Raleigh* (NC) *News and Observer* of May 25 adds...

> *...In the opening game, first inning home runs*
> *by Otis Foster and Danny Goins launched High*
> *Point on its way to victory...*

Writing in the May 25 edition of the *High Point Enterprise* under the byline "Panthers Punched From Area Playoffs," the article score reads...

> *...The Hilltoppers would go 10-36 in the game,*
> *with DeSantis collecting with three hits, Stacy*
> *and Kertes with 2 hits each, and Schmidt, Lufft,*
> *and West with one hit each. Girty would supply*
> *the lone rbi. In addition, the Hilltoppers left 11*
> *runners on base, while HPS would leave 7.*

Ray Searage would absorb the loss (5-3), while scattering nine hits, walking four and striking out 10. Following their first inning home runs, Foster and Goins would go 1-7 the remainder of the game.

"Hilltoppers Bow From Tournament" read the lead in the May 23 edition of the *Wheeling News Register*. The article went on to say…

Otis Foster, the NAIA's leading home run hitter in the nation, cracked a two-run blast and Danny Goins followed with another homer in the first inning which started High Point on its way to a 5-1 triumph over West Liberty here Saturday afternoon, eliminating the Hilltoppers from the NAIA Area 7 playoffs. The High Pointers, who now own a 42-5 record, went against the University of North Carolina-Wilmington Branch Saturday night in the championship game of the double-elimination event with the survivor moving on to St. Joseph, Mo., this week for the NAIA World Series. West Liberty came out of the event with a 1-2 tourney record. After beating Newberry in the opener on Thursday, the Hilltoppers had the misfortune to blow a 7-3 lead against Wilmington in the eighth inning of the rain-delayed Friday contest, finally losing by 8-7 with the winning run crossing the plate on a catcher's interference call with the bases loaded in the ninth. Lefty Ray Searage, who lost in relief on Friday, came back yesterday and went the distance. The freshman from Long Island did an excellent job after the shaky start and yielded only single runs in the fifth and seventh frames. Paul

173

Walker singled home High Point's tally in the fifth and Foster got an RBI single in the seventh. The Gold and Black's only run crossed the plate in the ninth. Tom Lufft doubled, moved to third on an error and scored on Girty's infield out. The defeat closed the Hilltoppers' season with a 20-15 record. Coach Jim Watson's was (sic) club was Northern Division champions for the fourth straight in the West Virginia Intercollegiate Conference and the 'Toppers have captured the overall league crown three straight years. Winning High Point hurler Delvin Idol scattered 10 hits and struck out two while walking three. Searage gave up just five hits and struck out 10. He issued four walks.

The Saturday match-up would see High Point College going against the University of North Carolina-Wilmington in the championship game. The Seahawks would defeat the Panthers 4-3 to advance to St. Joseph (MO) and the NAIA College World Series, where they would be eliminated in the second round of the competition. UNC-W baseball coach, Bill Brooks, would be named 1975 NAIA Coach of the Year.

Overall, the Hilltoppers would end the '75 season with 20 wins and 15 losses…a .571 percentage, and a 15-3 record in the WVIAC…an impressive .833 winning percentage.

1975 Final Results
WLSC Scores vs. Opponent Scores

3	UNC-W	4
3	Jacksonville U	9
6	Florida A&M U	2

3	Valdosta State College	4
	Columbus College	rained out
	Concord College	rained out
3	Marietta College	4
5	Davis & Elkins College	3
7	Davis and Elkins College	2
8	Morris Harvey College	0
2	Morris Harvey College	0
15	Glenville State College	1
1	Glenville State College	0
0	Salem State College	5
6	Salem State College	4
6	West Virginia University	8
4	West Virginia University	5
2	West Virginia State	5
3	West Virginia State	1
6	West Virginia Wesleyan Col.	0
7	West Virginia Wesleyan Col.	1
12	Fairmont State College	3
2	Fairmont State College	1
0	California State College	3
11	California State College	12
1	Alderson-Broaddus College	5
6	Alderson-Broaddus College	5
	Steubenville College	rained out
	Steubenville College	rained out
13	West Virginia Tech	6
10	West Virginia Tech	2
5	Frostburg State College	4
1	Frostburg State College	5
17		12
9	West Virginia State	1
5	West Virginia State	8
13	West Virginia State	5

Dr. Michael F. Price

10	Newberry College	5
7	UNC-Wilmington	8
1	High Point College	5
20		15

Final stats for the '75 team (regular season)
(Hitting)

Player	Games	At Bat	Hits	Average
DeMeo	6	8	3	.375
DeSantis	32	106	30	283
Duplaga	27	76	22	.289
Frey	16	34	9	.265
Girty	32	111	28	.252
Hynes	4	5	1	.250
Kertes	31	100	29	.290
Lufft	31	98	27	.276
Mellinger	30	81	26	.321
Price	10	12	2	.166
Schmidt	32	101	36	.356
Shepherd	1			
Spencer	14	18	1	.056
Stacy	32	117	38	.325
Vargo	1			
West	30	81	20	.247
Zaugg	4			
Total	**32**	**933**	**272**	**.290**

(Pitching)

Pitcher	Games	IP	W/L	ERA
Bonar	7	35 2/3	3-2	2.75
Dulkoski	3	6 2/3	0-2	6.75
Fabbro	8	23 2/3	1-2	3.42
Freshwater	8	65 2/3	6-2	2.60

Searage	8	45 1/3	5-1	5.56
Williams	9	72	4-4	2.75
Total	**32**	**239**	**19-13**	**3.42**

Opposing Teams' Batting Average .206

The team's impressive conference record would be enough to land three Hilltoppers on the twelve-member, all-conference team, including Robbie Schmidt, Mark Stacy, and Gary Freshwater. The Special Honorable Mention would land two players, Dave Williams and Jon Kertes. At the same time, the Honorable Mention list adds Jim Mellinger, Ray Searage, and Tom Lufft. Of the forty-four total selections on the all-conference list, a West Liberty player's name would be chosen in nearly one-in-every-five of the selections.

Regarding the all-conference selection, Nick Bedway, Associate Sports Editor, would add in the May 23 edition of the *Wheeling News-Register* entitled "3 Hilltoppers On All-League," that…

…A four-year veteran, Schmidt is enjoying his most productive season for the Hilltoppers… The ex-Wheeling Wildcat ranks as the top Hilltopper hitter, pounding out 36 hits in 101 at bats for a .356 average. He collected eight home runs and had 29 RBI's…This was a comeback year for the smooth-fielding Stacy who missed all of last season because of about with mononucleosis. He batted .319 with 31 hits in 97 at bats and handled the second bases duties almost flawlessly. The rangy Freshwater, who stands 6-3, went into this weekend's action with a 6-2 pitching record, racking up 44 strikeouts in 46 innings and allowing only 34 hits while compiling a 1.54 ERA.

Dr. Michael F. Price

According to the May 25 edition of the *Bluefield Daily Telegram,*

...Rob Schmidt, senior first baseman from
Wheeling, led the Liberty attack at the plate.
In 101 trips, he punched out 36 hits, including
eight home runs, for a .346 (sic) average.
Schmidt, who batted .349 his junior year,
moved up from the Honorable Mention list of
last season. Mark Stacy, rookie second baseman
from Steubenville, Ohio, proved to be a great
pivot on the double play and extremely
reliable as a hitter. The freshman infielder
successfully hit 31 times for a .319 (sic)
average. Gary Freshwater, 6'3" pitcher, led
the West Liberty mound corp. The 21-year
old junior from Colliers, West Virginia, ended
the regular season with a 6-1 record. In 46
innings pitched, the opponents went down
swinging 44 times while he allowed only 34
hits for an excellent 1.54 ERA.

Beyond the three players that West Liberty placed on the 12-member, All-WVIAC team, the selections included two players each from Alderson-Broaddus, Morris Harvey, Salem, and West Virginia State. West Virginia Wesleyan freshman pitcher, Scott Koepka, completed the roster and was also chosen as "Pitcher of the Year." Mike Lewis from West Virginia State led the league in hitting and was selected as the "Hitter of the Year." The All-Conference team comprised five seniors, two juniors, three sophomores, and two freshmen, one of whom was Mark Stacy.

Just as the season had come to a close, so, too, were things around the campus shutting down. However, there were some last-minute news items. The cafeterias at Krise

178

Hall and Rogers Hall were pleading with students to please return all borrowed silverware and glassware ASAP. Among the crowd that day as Dr. Norman Dixon, professor at the University of Pittsburgh, addressed the nearly 380 graduating seniors at the 139th year of commencement on May 11, were baseball players Jon Kertes and Dave Williams who were receiving their diplomas.

Dave Williams

Citing Dave's accomplishments, *The Tribune* (Coshocton, OH) of June 10, writes…

> *David J. Williams, received a bachelor of science degree in business administration during the spring commencement ceremonies recently at West Liberty State College in Wheeling, West. Va…Williams was a four-year letterman on the West Liberty baseball team and was nominated to receive the 'Mr. Hilltopper' award, presented to the outstanding young man on campus…*

And speaking of baseball, the numbers indicate that the baseball team members ended the spring semester with a team grade point average of over 2.5.

179

Dr. Michael F. Price

Extra Inning

Baseball been berry, berry good to me.
(Chico Escuela/Garrett Morris)

To this point in the book, the writer has endeavored to do several things.

First, I wanted to show in general terms the rich history that lies behind the oldest public college in the state of West Virginia. In like manner, I also wanted to show how the school has evolved from its beginnings in 1837 to what it looks like nearly a century-and-a-half later. Along that same line, I tried to lift up several of the individuals that have provided guidance and leadership over the years and the policies that have come to shape student life.

Next, I wanted to show what student life was like at the school over the years. In particular, I wanted to highlight the school's efforts to create community while fostering an environment that advances students' intellectual, social, and emotional growth.

A third thing that I wanted to do was to provide a small slice of what life was like for a student-athlete. In this case, it is the nine months in the life of players on the West Liberty baseball team, and what went on between our arrival on campus in the fall of 1974 and when we last left the field in spring 1975. Specifically, I wanted to share the rigors of what it was like for a player on the baseball team as we went about balancing the demands of the classroom with the demands on the field.

Finally, I wanted to show the individual achievements of some very gifted players and the group accomplishments of an outstanding team, as seen through the spectrum of both players and the print media.

My prayer is that I have done all this with clarity, honesty, and justice. Anything less, and I have brought disrespect to the school, its leadership, the baseball program, myself, and the players that made that '75 season so special for me and so many of my teammates.

But to stop now is to literally stop at second base with no intent of scoring. It just wouldn't be right! This said, the remaining pages of this book could well be some of the most important. The pages that follow are some of the lessons learned that memorable season and how these lessons have transformed many of my teammates' lives once we left the field after that '75 season.

Among the first lessons learned during *The Season That Was* is a lesson on *accountability*.

Look at it like this. Technically speaking, an umpire will usually call a strike when a baseball being delivered by the pitcher does two things. The first thing is that the ball is thrown in the area between a batter's knees and the middle of his jersey. Just as important, the baseball must simultaneously cross that white, 17x8.5x12 inch irregular pentagon called home plate. When these two things happen simultaneously, the umpire will usually, emphasis on usually, call a strike on the batter. Apologies to all the baseball people, but I feel it's necessary to define a strike for all the non-baseball people reading this book. Now, where was I? Oh, yes, I remember…

However, what sometimes happens is that the batter will swing at a pitch that's outside the strike zone. When this happens, the batter is said to "widen" the strike zone. The purpose of the strike zone is to not only put some boundaries on pitches but also to keep things orderly and dignified. Such is the case with accountability. It's a necessity in life because individuals need boundaries in life to keep things orderly. The last thing a student-athlete wants to do is to go outside the boundaries and bring disrespect to teammates and the school. Albeit unwritten, the message from day one when my teammates and I first walked on that baseball field in August 1974 was that each of us is accountable for our actions.

We are accountable for the decisions we make and how we conduct ourselves on the field, in the dugout, in the classroom, in the cafeteria, and every place in-between. When players act with maturity and common sense, it shines a positive light on the team. Conversely, when a player's actions are not-so-good, it reflects poorly on the team and the school, because people will naturally connect the team and the school with the player.

Above all, the players on the team knew they were most accountable to themselves. Not once during the '75 season do I remember a player calling out another player for making an error, missing a sign, or not getting a hit. More than anyone, the player knew he had messed up, and he didn't need anyone to bring it to his attention. Accountability has nothing to do with placing blame, and everything to do with individual responsibility.

Coach Watson may never have said it, but he expected...no demanded...accountability from each of his twenty-four players. Coach conducted himself on and off the field with dignity, integrity, and decorum, and he expected the same from those that put on the West Liberty uniform. Some of the players may even go as far as to say that it was accountability that genuinely made the '75 team a good team, on and off the field. Whatever the case or the situation, Coach Watson modeled the behaviors he wanted to see in his players. Anything to the contrary would only widen the strike zone.

Equally as important was a lesson on *acceptance*.

To say that there was diversity on the '75 team would be an understatement. The members of the group came from big schools and small ones. Some of the guys participated in three or four sports during their high school days, while others played only baseball. The players on the 24-man roster came from blue-collar, middle-class households where the father worked in the steel mill, drove a truck, sold insurance, ran a convenient store, worked in manufacturing or maintenance, or owned a club. While most of the players on the team came from a two-parent household where the mother stayed at home, there were no less than four players that came from families where there was only one parent. More, there were two of the players that had graduated from military school, two who had a father or brother who had served in the military, and one player that was coming off a six-year stint in the Air Force. A few of the players had the opportunity of enrolling at West Liberty and not having to worry about finances.

In contrast, there were others that would not have been able to attend West Liberty if not for work-study, student loans, and government grants. There were just as many that lived off-campus and were in a fraternity as lived in dorms and considered the members of the baseball team to be their fraternity. Above all, it seems that very few of the players were recruited by other colleges, which meant that most trying out for the team were walk-on prospects who simply wanted to play baseball at West Liberty. Without question, the economic, social, and financial differences that were so prevalent opened the eyes of many of the players to a world that was vastly different from their own.

And through it all, it was Coach Watson that forged the concept that acceptance and inclusion are paramount if there was to be unity on the team. Subsequently, the coach urged the players to informally mingle so they could get to know each other. He encouraged first-year players to make an effort to know the returning players, upperclassmen to interact with freshmen, and so on. Coach Watson persuaded

pitchers to hang out with infielders, outfielders to get to
know catchers, and regular players to know the bench guys.
More, he systematically labored to make it happen.

On away games, when the team had to stay overnight, it
was not uncommon for the coach to change up room
assignments, so players were seldom with the same players
they had roomed with before. By the time the season had
ended, Coach Watson had shown his masterful skill at not
only navigating the rough waters of athletic egotism, social
and economic differences, and skill levels of the players, but
was also successful in getting the players to buy into the
concept that the team is one family.

In an article entitled "It's 'All in the Family' for WLS
Diamond Nine," Doug Huff, Associate Sports Editor with
the *Wheeling Intelligencer*, had some glowing words to say
about Coach Watsons's unique talent to both bridge the
differences that were so apparent among his '75 players, and
at the same time, advance harmony and oneness.

*When West Liberty State employed a bachelor
baseball coach-athletic trainer four years
ago, it obviously didn't figure on getting a
"family man." But that's exactly how it turned
out-much to the delight of the Hilltopper athletic
program. Jim Watson has turned the WLS
baseball squad into the 'team to beat'...and
has achieved this goal with the close-knit
"family" approach. You see, Jim's campus
"family" is the baseball team in particular and
the athletic program in general. The highly-
successful, youth mentor-who could pass as one
of his own players-fosters the idea that unity
and cohesiveness are key ingredients in any
successful team sport. That's why he can be
found on and off campus with his players
attending a prep game, socializing, or just*

hanging out. Jim Watson is more than just a coach…he's one of the boys. There's no generation or communication gap in this diamond "family." And his approach to the game has reaped more than its share of rewards…It's a family affair for Jim Watson…

———————

Equally as important as the lessons of accountability and acceptance, the players learned the importance of proper *time-management.*

Looking beyond the spring trip, the '75 baseball team actually played in twenty-eight games between the March 27 game with Marietta College, and the May 11, WVIAC championship game, against West Virginia State. This adds up to over three-hundred-and-seventy innings of baseball. Of those twenty-eight games, all but two were doubleheaders, and half of the twenty-eight games were road games, including trips to Marietta, OH; Charleston twice, Glenville, Institute, Fairmont, and Philippi, WV; and California, PA. This is to say nothing about actual travel time to and from the away games. Further, nine of the twenty-eight games were weekday games, while seven were played on the weekend. The remaining games were all home games, with four being weekday games and four being played on the weekend. Clearly, the demanding schedule meant the players must learn to use every opportunity presented to them to complete homework, prepare for an upcoming test or catch-up on reading assignments.

One of the biggest venues that players utilized to stay current with their schoolwork was to do their work in one of the two, five-row, 15-seat, team vans while traveling to away games. It was pretty much a tradition. The van driver and a co-pilot would occupy the front two seats, leaving the remaining four rows of seats open. However, it was an unwritten rule that if a player had classwork to do, he would sit in the second row since it was the quietest row next to the driver's row. The last two rows in the van were for those players that wanted to play cards, usually spades or crazy eights. The third row of seats acted as the "buffer row," and those that sat there just wanted to usually sit and look out the windows or sleep.

The point is exact: the players seemed to have a small window of time to complete classwork once the '75 season began. Either the players learn to use every spare minute they could for schoolwork, or else time would eventually get the best of them. Additionally, many of the players unknowingly gained the distinctive skill to balance many things at once, to prioritize what's essential over less important things, and to decide what deserves their full attention and energies and what is down the list and can wait.

Another lesson that was learned that special season, and has since been adopted in the lives of many of the players, is the understanding that we *all have a role in life.*

The responsibility of the leadoff hitter is, first and foremost, to get on base. The lead-off batter figuratively "sets the table" for the players that follow. It is the duty of the second batter in the line up to move the lead-off batter to the next base and, possibly, beyond. The task of the following three batters, hitters three, four, and five in the line-up, is to make sure that whoever is on base scores. These three batters are crucial to a team scoring runs, and that's why they are commonly referred to as the "heart of the order." As for batters six, seven, and eight, they are to do whatever it takes to keep things going, walk, sacrifice, or get a hit. As for the number nine hitter, the pitcher, their job, well, is to pitch and not so much to hit. When there's a designated hitter in the line-up in place of the pitcher hitting, the job of the number nine hitter is to be a second lead-off batter. In most cases, the last batter is in the game more for their glove than their bat. Without a doubt, every player in the line-up has a role when it comes to hitting, and each was just as valuable as the others. For any player that wants to contribute, the key is for that player to find their role on the team.

I was not what one might call a good hitter, and by most standards, I was only slightly above average as an outfielder. However, there were two things that I was above-average at…running fast and bunting…and that became my role on the '75 team…bunt, and run for the catcher when called upon to do so. Occasionally my freshman year, I would be called upon to play in the outfield when there was no fence, and, of course, I batted last in the line-up. However, bunting and running became my role, and I accepted it for the good of the team. And when I realized that I was included on the roster for a specific purpose and role, the season became much more enjoyable. I was honored to be called upon in particular situations, and I was elated when I did my job well and contributed to the success of the team. And so it is in life.

Our goal should be directed at discovering our role and purpose in life, and then to perform that role with integrity and honor. If we sense our skills are to teach, we should teach with total commitment, conviction, and dedication. If we feel our role in life is to be a salesperson, an administrator, a coach, husband, father, or grandfather, our goal is to be the best we can be! And if we not only find our role in life but also carry out that role to the best of our abilities, we will have made a positive contribution in the life, or lives, of others, regardless if we're in the lead-off spot or last in the line-up.

A fifth lesson that was learned during *The Season That Was* and has since found its way into the lives of many of the players centers on *respect*.

Dr. Michael F. Price

The game of baseball is played in a very defined area with very defined factors. In large part, the game is played with four bases being 90-feet apart, the pitcher's mound being 60-feet, six inches away from home plate, and the distance from the back tip of home plate to second base is 127-feet, 3 and 3/8 inches. Additionally, the distance from home plate to the outfield fence in right and left field commonly runs between 310-feet and 325-feet. The fence in centerfield is usually 400 to 410-feet away from home plate. As for a player's bat, it cannot exceed a specific size and weight, and the baseball must weigh no more than 5 ¼ ounces or exceed 9 ¼ inches in circumference. Even a player's gloves have specifications as to size.

In the same way, there are written rules that govern the game, including how someone appeals a specific play, how many warm-up pitches a pitcher gets once he enters the game, when is a hit really a hit, and under what conditions can a game be delayed or canceled. There are even written rules that pertain to when a player or coach can call time out, how many bases a runner can advance when the ball becomes stuck in either the catcher or the umpire's mask, and one that says a pitcher can switch their throwing arm when pitching to a batter if the pitcher believes they have injured their other arm.

Just as numerous are the unwritten rules of baseball. For one, a player never walks in front of the home plate umpire on his way to the batter's box. Similarly, a player should never try to hurt or show up a player on the other team, stand in the batter's box and watch after they hit a home run, talk to a pitcher who is throwing a no-hitter, or treat a team that's 0-8 with less regard than facing a team that's 8-0.

The game of baseball is simple: you hit the ball, you run the bases, and you catch the ball. And all the action in baseball takes place inside the fence, with the vast majority happening between the first and third base lines.

It's a different story, however, once a player is outside the fences. There, as most can attest, life is not lived according to some succinctly defined black and white rules found in a 4x6 inch paperback book. Outside the fences, life is defined more by relationships than by rules, more by caring and compassion than by a call of out or safe, and more by "how" can we help rather than "if" we should help. Coach Watson insisted that his players conduct themselves outside the fence in the same way they did when they were inside the fence. That was with character and respect. In the long run, life is more significant than baseball to Coach Watson.

In life, there are no fences, but doing the little things in life are just as important and meaningful as are the little things in baseball. A kind word here, a little compassion there, or a simple act of caring, can sometimes be just as impactful as hitting a 2-run homer in the bottom of the ninth when the team is losing by one run, or making a diving catch with the team up by one run. Clearly, to Coach Watson, life is more than a nine-inning game or a doubleheader played inside the fences. Instead, it's a game that takes place outside the fences and involves extra innings. The most significant rule, written or unwritten, is that respect will be extended when respect is given.

––––––––––

Last but not least, the special season of '75 taught most players *patience*.

Playing time during the season was not spread equally, mostly since there were 11 returning lettermen from the '74 team that was 16-9 overall and 12-5 in the conference, captured the WVIAC championship trophy for the second year in a row and participated in the Area 7 tournament in as many years. Of these eleven players, two returning players were all-conference, and five were all-conference honorable mention. If one excludes the all-conference pitcher, this means that six of the nine regular positions on the field were "already filled." Consequently, highly-gifted players, first-year guys who were regulars on their high school team, suddenly found themselves as situational players and with little playing time during the '75 season.

Of the six non-pitchers that were new to the '75 team and were not part of the regular line-up, they appeared in a combined 51 games, had 72 at-bats, scored 23 runs, had 15 hits, and knocked in 10 runs in total. In contrast, the five returning players selected to the '74 all-conference team appeared in a combined 157 games, had nearly 500 at-bats, crossed home 110 times, had a combined 149 hits, and had about 90 RBI's in the '75 season. Subsequently, patience became the name of the game for these newer players. They knew their time on the field would come. Until then, they continued to practice with the team, ride for hours to away games and see little, if any, playing time, and anxiously wait for their turn to get on the field or in the batter's box.

And yet, one would guess that these players are probably some of the most patient, calm, and persistent individuals in their adult lives. While patience can be a virtue, it is not easy. Yet, patient people are some of the most understanding, reflective, and compassionate people in society. If life truly is more of a marathon than a sprint, then most guys on the '75 team are adequately prepared for whatever lies ahead for them in life.

And never have these lessons in accountability, acceptance, finding our role in life, respect, and patience, become more defined, widely practiced, and incorporated than they have in the lives of those 24 players once they walked off the West Liberty baseball field for the last time.

How did that special season transform the lives of many of these players? In their own words and in no particular order...

After graduating in 1976, my brother Randy and I purchased the gas station previously owned by my father in 1977, the same year I married Connie Warren, whom I met at WL. I bought my first house that year for 19,000.00. We had our first child, Tracy in 1979 and our second child, Jamie in 1981. Todd was an added blessing coming in 1993. All are married and I have 4 grandchildren.

Just an interjection, after I had children, I knew the blessing and responsibility that was on me. I vowed from then on I would never curse in front of my children and try my best, with the help of God, to set a good example for my kids.

Connie was a stay at home mom, which I am so thankful for.

I continued to play baseball with the Warwood Reds from 1975 until 1993 approximately, at which time I badly sprained my ankle and figured it was time to quit. That was a very enjoyable time for me because the foundation of that team were players that I either played with at WL or they were talented local players who played at other colleges. We participated in 1975 and 76 in the NBC national tournament and won both state championships before being eliminated in the regional tournaments after winning the first game.

I continued working with my brother, purchasing property and building a 5 bay service garage next to the gas station in 1999. In 2007 we purchased the gas station next to us and torn it down, expanding our current station. In 2012, I bought the business from my brother and am currently running it with my son and daughter.

I am so grateful to have grown up in the time that we did and knowing all of you. I pray every day that our kids and grandkids will have the same opportunities and futures that we have enjoyed. But God only knows that future.

I hope the difficulties that all of us will eventually face will never take away from the memories we have.

(*Robbie Schmidt*)

Dr. Michael F. Price

After West Liberty, I went to work for a national fundraising company called Nasco Inc., out of Springfield, Tennessee. At that time, they had over 300 reps, but I was fortunate enough to be in the top 10 each year that I was with them. In 1990, I decided to start my own fundraising company called Unique School Sales. We are still in business today and have been blessed with good success.

In 1980, I married my best friend and the most beautiful girl at West Liberty, Denise. We just celebrated 40-years of marriage and are still going strong. We raised two strong young men, Jason, now 37, and Jonathan is now 32. Denise has a master's degree in elementary education, did some teaching, and was a Children's Pastor for 12-years. However, she stayed home for 18-years to raise our boys. Both of our boys own their own businesses.

We are blessed with three amazing grandkids, Jason and Hillary have one daughter name Eliana, and Jonathan and Elaine have two boys, Jameson and Samuel.

Denise and I attribute our success in business, marriage, and raising a family to our faith in Christ. Without Him, none of this would've been possible!

My Business Management degree at West Liberty, along with the opportunity to play baseball for two-years under a great Coach Watson and with a bunch of great guys, provided me a solid foundation to get me jumpstarted in life. If I could, I would go back there and do it all over again.

(Rick DeMeo)

After school, I really was not sure what direction I was interested in pursuing career-wise. I took a couple of jobs in retail, then insurance, but neither interested me. My opportunity came when I accepted a job with Capitol Mfg. in Columbus, Ohio, an inside sales position. I knew then that I wanted to be in industrial sales, preferably as an outside sales/account manager. Being young, single, and cheap, I transferred to Houston, TX, essentially handling inside sales and warehouse manager position.

During this time, I met my future wife, Janice, who was working in the same industry. Janice was from Tulsa, and I traveled with her up there on vacation. As a West Virginian, I liked two-lane roads, and Tulsa was more my style, so off we went.

We got married on October 25, 1980, and I continued working for valve manufacturers as an area manager through 1989 when I accepted a promotion to move back to Houston with Worcester Controls.

During this time, my oldest daughter Kristin and youngest, Kara, were born in 1982 and 1985.

The biggest break of my working career was in 1994 when I went to work for The Eads Company as an account manager covering the oil and gas market. Eads was a manufacturers rep/distributor of valves, instrumentation, filtration, and plant specialty equipment. Sales went very well, and in 2000, I had the opportunity to buy in as a part-owner. We took it from $60 million in sales to over $140 million in 10-years with no debt. In 2012, we sold 70% to a private investment company, which was very lucrative. Seven years later, we sold the last 30% to FCX/AIT, and our ownership of the company ended. I retired on August 2, 2019, after 25-years with the company.

On the personal front, I have been married to my lovely wife and best friend, Janice, for 40-years. I have two great daughters, Kristin and Kara, 5 awesome grandkids, Emma, James, Evan, Thomas, and Colin. My infield is almost set!

I played baseball in a number of independent leagues until I was close to 30, with good success. Still enjoyed the competition. I also had the honor of being inducted into my high school hall of fame (Brooke High) in 2008.

Nowadays, I work out, play golf, and play a little ball with the grandkids.

I feel very blessed with my life. A great marriage, kids, and grandkids, but I will never forget the fun, competition, and mission we were on in 1975. It was a great time of my life, and I am honored to have been a part of it.

(Gary Freshwater)

After graduating from WLSC in 1978, I returned to Central Ohio and began building new memories with my college sweetheart, Beth McVicker. We were married in August of 1978 (just 2 months after graduation) and started our lives in New Comerstown, Ohio.

Beth graduated from WLSC with a Degree in Dental Hygiene. She worked as a Dental Hygienist for 40-years, finally retiring in 2018. I graduated from WLSC with a General Business Degree - working in Safety Sales Industry from 1980 through the present.

A couple months after we were married, I found my first solid employment with Edmont-Wilson (Coshocton, Ohio), now known as Ansell. This is the first of three major jobs that I will have worked until my retirement. This new adventure put me in a position to start my professional sales career. After two years working as a sales trainee in Coshocton, Ohio, I transferred to Buffalo, NY, as a Sales Territory Manager covering western New York. Nine years into that position, I accepted a similar position with Ansell, relocating to Cincinnati, OH. I would work another nine-years with Ansell covering southern Ohio and the Kentucky sales market as a Territory Manager.

The year 1995 brought me a great opportunity to become a co-founder of a new start-up manufacturing representative business servicing the safety industry. With my partner and good friend, Denny Swigert, we opened our doors under the name of Targeting Customer Safety, Inc. (TCS, INC). Our new jobs allowed us to represent and promote small, medium, and large safety manufacturers into the industrial safety field. This new business and its opportunity grew rapidly. Nine years passed quickly when a management opportunity at Best Glove Manufacturing in Menlo, GA, opened up in 2004.

The year 2004 turned out to be another interesting year and a new adventure for my family and me. Best Glove, now the Showa Group, offered me a Regional Sales Manager's position covering the East coast. The timing was great, as all three of my children had graduated high school and were either married, in college, and of course, living on their own. In December of 2004, I started my new position as their Eastern Regional Manager. As of this writing, I'm still working with the Showa Group as a Regional Sales manager – just now entering the middle of my 16th year.

Our children have brought us great joy over our 42-years of life together: Megan Zaugg (Grosz) is our oldest and currently resides in Sanford, Florida, with two of our six grandchildren, London and Hayden. Megan is VP of Sales and Marketing for Omega Imaging Corporation and is a graduate of the University of Cincinnati. Our son, Drew, currently resides in Cincinnati, Ohio, with his wife Becky, and their two children, Ellie and Zoe. Becky is employed by Accenture, and Drew is currently employed by Airgas as a Sales Account Manager. Drew and Becky are both graduates of Xavier University. Our other daughter, Erinn Zaugg (Grunkemeyer), currently resides in Cincinnati with her husband Peter, and their two children, Henry and Ada. Currently, Erinn works as the nurse for Anderson Ohio Middle School and the University of Cincinnati Hospital labor and delivery team. Peter works in sales with his father in their manufacturing representative business. Erinn is a graduate of Ohio University and Christ Hospital School of Nursing Program, while Peter is a graduate of the University of Cincinnati.Beth and I enjoy traveling. We have been very blessed to visit numerous countries, beaches, and islands. We belong to the Newtown, Ohio, United Methodist Church, and our favorite place to vacation in the United States would be the beaches at Hilton Head Island, SC. Our future plans are to continue to build our memories with our children and grandchildren and travel in the United States. It is hard to imagine that a decision made back in 1974 to attend West Liberty State College provided me with my loving wife of 42-years, three wonderful children, six adorable grand-children, a very successful career in sales, and a lifetime connection to a baseball dynasty.

Special thanks to Coach Watson, my teammates for all 4-years, my friends, and families that help made me grow from a shy 18-year-old to who I am today. Coach Watson, his support staff, and my teammates provided me with the strength, knowledge, and confidence to raise my family with love and respect.

(Steve Zaugg)

After graduating in 1978 with a business degree, I was the owner/operator of a Convenient Food Mart franchise for nineteen years. I sold my business and building and got certified to teach business in high school. I worked for six years as a teacher at Steubenville High School. For the last twenty years, I have worked as a court bailiff and probation officer at Steubenville Municipal Court for two judges.

I credit baseball as a pathway to college and giving me a chance to mentor hundreds of "sons" over the past 33 years. I served as a coach for 33-years for Steubenville American Legion baseball, serving as Manager for 12 of those years. During those 33-years, our teams won six state titles. During that same period, I served as an assistant coach at Steubenville High School for 21 years.

I have coached seven players that have gone on to play professionally with two playing Major League Baseball and one quarterbacking his team to a Grey Cup in the Canadian Football League. I had the pleasure to coach 41 Division I baseball players and countless other players who played in college. In 2011, I was inducted into the West Liberty Athletic Hall of Fame, and in 2016 was a Franciscan University of Steubenville Baron Club Award winner for my contributions to my community through baseball.

My wife, Joan, a retired nurse, and I have two daughters, Julie and Jenna. Julie is a Kindergarten teacher. Jenna is also a Kindergarten teacher and the Cheerleading Coach at Youngstown State University. In addition, we have six grandchildren. Joan and I currently reside in Steubenville, Ohio.

(Mark Stacy)

———————

Following my graduation from West Liberty in 1978, I enrolled in graduate school at West Virginia University. Even though I spent much of the 1979-80 school year dealing with a case of mononucleosis, I was still able to finish my classwork and ended up receiving my MA in American History in the summer of 1981. In August of that same year, I entered the seminary at Brite Divinity School, Texas Christian University, in Ft. Worth, Texas.

Between graduating from Brite in 1986, taking my first church, and now, I have served seven congregations in five states, and in two different denominations. With a desire to earn my doctorate, I was accepted in 1995 into graduate school at George Washington University in Washington, DC. Four years later, I graduated with a doctorate in Education.

It was while I was serving a church in North Carolina in 2006 that I began teaching college at Mt. Olive College, now the University of Mt. Olive. For the next eight years, I had the honor of teaching several subjects, including Old and

Dr. Michael F. Price

New Testament, American History, and Historical Geography. In 2012, I also began teaching classes for North Carolina Wesleyan College World and Near East Religions.

In between all of this, I have written three books: *How to Manage Money Like a Minister* (2009), *Murder on the Disoriented Express: How Laity May Be Killing Their Congregation* (2019), and *Backfill: How the Latter Gospel Writers Transformed the Historical Jesus into the Risen Christ* (2020), run with the bulls in Pamplona, Spain; walked Pickett's Charge at Gettysburg National Battlefield; run over and cruised under the Skyway Bridge in St. Petersburg, Florida; and preached on countless occasions at The Tabernacle on Martha's Vineyard, MA.

I have been married to my wife, Betty, for 12-years. Between us, we have five children: Rodney Smith, who runs his own computer business in Raleigh, NC; Jason Lydon, who works for a large alcohol distributorship on the east coast, and lives in Delaware with his wife, Tiffany, and their two sons, Cormac and Seamus; Dr. Zachary Price, a chiropractor in Charlotte, NC, who is married to Laurin, and they have a baby girl named Berkley (KiKi) Grace; Joshua Price, a member of the PGA and the Assistant Pro at the Cabarrus Country Club in Charlotte, and Hannah Rose (Price) Dilday, a stay-at-home mom who lives in Raleigh, NC, with her husband, Brad, and their three girls: Rosemary (Nabby), Tillman Grace (Muffin), and the newest edition to the household, Wynn Elizabeth (Pepper).

I retired from ministry in 2020, and Betty and I call Largo, FL, home.

(Michael Price)

I am very proud of my career and the accomplishments of my children and wife. I attribute a big part of my success to West Liberty State College. The school prepared me academically for my future, and the baseball team and Coach

Watson prepared me as an athlete and a person. Playing baseball at West Liberty State College was an honor and I will always cherish the friendships and memories. Thank you to all of my teammates.

I graduated from West Liberty State College in May 1978. Upon graduation, I worked for Harbison-Walker Refractories in the Marketing Department, and on July 7, 1979, I married Mikie (Michelle) Frey. She and I met at the age of 12 in 7th grade. We were best friends through our senior year but never dated. It was only after entering West Liberty my freshman year that we began dating. We have been married for 41-years.

Six months after we married, I got a job at Youngstown Hospital Association as the Assistant Director of Purchasing.

On August 18, 1982, my first child Jaime Richelle Frey was born! She was a competitive dancer and a cheerleader growing up. Currently, she is a teacher in the Aurora Ohio school system. She has blessed our lives with two beautiful grandchildren, Tenley Grace and Bennett Alan.

In May of 1983, I took a position at Marymount Hospital as the Director of Materials Management. While I was there, I started a golf league, bowling league, and coached the hospital softball teams.

On September 8, 1985, my son Craig Branton Frey was born. He was born with a bat in his crib at the hospital. He began ice hockey at three-years-old and baseball and golf soon followed. He was recruited to play baseball at Furman University but chose to go to Washington and Jefferson College's pre-med program and is a physician.

My last child, Taylor Leigh Frey, was born on April 21, 1990, and is currently a teacher in Maryland. She gave us many years of fun as an accomplished soccer player, gymnast, and cheerleader.

Dr. Michael F. Price

Much of our time throughout the years was spent with dance recitals, football and basketball cheerleading, hockey games, golf matches, and baseball throughout the country.

I am retired from the Cleveland Clinic as an Administrator for the Children's Hospital, but currently the Administrator for my son's physician practice. My wife is still teaching 1st grade.

(Rich Frey)

After WLU, I worked at Grocers Development Corp. in Wheeling, building and operating Convenient Food Mart Stores in the Tri-State Area. I married in 1979 to Mary DiCarlantonio, from Steubenville, OH. I was elected to the Brooke County Commission in 1983 and left to become President of Silver Franchising in Fredericksburg, VA, in 1988.

I remained there until 1993 and then repurchased the company that franchised all of the Convenient Food Marts. I sold that company in 2017 and am currently the COO of the Silver Companies in Boca Raton, FL. In 2014, I was inducted into the West Liberty Athletic Hall of Fame.

My wife and I live in Wellington, FL. We had 3 children. Tony is a Director of IT for Advent Hospitals located in Altamonte Springs, FL, and they have 4 children. Our daughter, Alyssa, is Director of Human Resources for PepsiCo., located in Pittsburgh. She was married last September. Our son, Franco, passed away in 1990 due to complications of cancer.

Our life is good. I shot an 81 yesterday, the best round of golf I ever played.

(Gregg DeSantis)

It was indeed an honor to be a part of the West Liberty State College baseball program. The time I spent with the team helped me learn how to handle life situations and grow into the person I have become today.

During the fall of 1975, I made the difficult decision to leave the West Liberty's baseball program to pursue refereeing in the parochial basketball league. My late cousin, Darwin Jones, was quite influential in this choice, as he had been a baseball umpire and provided guidance and encouragement in this direction. Little did I know at the time that this was the beginning of what would become a 45-year professional refereeing career that came to a close this past New Year's Eve while officiating the Liberty Bowl football game in Memphis, Tennessee. Navy beat Kansas State on a last-second field goal; it was an exciting end to a treasured career! During this time, I traveled across the United States, working college football, basketball, and baseball games.

While officiating, I also worked for 14 years as an educator. Two of those years were spent as the Principal/Athletic Director of Bishop Donahue High School. I also taught business courses, Algebra, and other mathematics classes. My teaching career was rounded out by coaching girls' basketball, track, and football at Union Junior High in Benwood, WV.

I eventually left the education field and joined corporate America, which led me to my current position as Executive Director of Safety and Risk at PGT Trucking, Inc. in Aliquippa, PA. I continue to enjoy coaching and teaching the staff of this ever-changing field and building team success. I am very blessed to have had the ability to juggle officiating and with my valuable PGT career.

I am married to Lisa, my best friend in life, and she has inspired me to continue my pursuit of excellence each and every day. We enjoy working out and watching college and professional football together. My adopted daughter Jenna and Lisa's daughter Amber bring great joy to us as well. I

Dr. Michael F. Price

had the honor of walking Jenna halfway down the aisle last summer at her wedding!

(Paul Vargo)

Following the '75 season, I played baseball in the Steubenville area for about a month or two. It was during that time that I received a call from a friend in Los Angeles to come to California and play winter league with the Baltimore Orioles minor leaguers. In 1976, I was invited to play summer ball and later signed to play with the Victoria (TX) Cowboys in the Class A, Gulf States League. I played about a half of a season and was released.

I went back to California in the fall of that year, and with a friend of mine, got a union job as a carpenter. For the next 6 years, I worked as an employee to a large construction firm.

In 1982, I passed the test to become a licensed general contractor. Shortly after that, I began my own construction company, Jon Kertes Construction (funny note: I now make more money in one day than I did for one whole month playing baseball. Sad what we made in the 70s.).

Got radically salvation in 1977, and married my wife, Judy, in 1982. We have been married for nearly 40-years and have three grown children: Julianne, a sociologist by training, but currently works outside the field in marketing; Jonathan, who is a vice president and works for a construction company in field operations; and Jennifer, our youngest, who works in the nursing field.

Over the years, I have developed three inventions. In 2004, I created a self-propelled scooter that rewinds itself as it is being used. The following year I invented an onboard safety detection and warning device that lets drivers know another vehicle is beside them. Also, in 2005, I designed an illuminated scooter that runs on stored-up energy. All three of the inventions have been patented.

I have had the opportunity to travel to many countries and states to build and preach the gospel of Jesus Christ.

My wish and prayer are that all the old buddies of the '75 Hilltoppers would also come to the saving knowledge of Jesus Christ. Best decision in my life.

(Jon Kertes)

———

Following the '76 season in which I was named to the WVIAC all-conference team and "Pitcher of the Year," I was drafted by the St. Louis Cardinals. After a few years in the minors, I was traded to the Mets organization and made my major league debut in June 1981. During the brief time with the Mets, I won my first game and got my first major league hit, giving me the distinction of being the only player in the Met's organization to have a 100% winning percentage and bat a thousand. In the years that followed, I had the honor of playing for the Cleveland Indians, Milwaukee Brewers, Chicago White Sox, and finished my playing career in 1990 with the Los Angeles Dodgers. During my seven years in the majors, I appeared in over 250 games and pitched in nearly 300 innings, mainly in a relief role.

In 1994, I was contacted by St. Louis Cardinal management with an offer to become the pitching coach of the Madison Hatters, their Class A team in the Midwest League. This officially began my coaching career. Since then, I have worked with several organizations and through several levels of baseball, including the Prince William Cannons of the Carolina League and the Orlando Rays of the Southern League, and the Florida Marlins.

Beginning in 2003, I landed with the Pirates organization. I coached their teams in the NY-Penn League, South Atlantic League, Class AA Eastern League, and the Class AAA League. In October 2009, I became the assistant pitching coach for the Pittsburgh Pirates and was named interim pitching coach for the club the following year. When

203

Dr. Michael F. Price

Clint Hurdle was named the Pirate manager in 2010, I was named the full-time pitching coach. After being involved for 41-years as a pitcher and a coach, I left baseball at the close of the 2019 season.

In 2013, I was not only awarded an honorary Doctor of Humane Letters, but I also had the honor of delivering the commencement speech for the graduating class of the fall term. I am equally honored to be a member of the West Liberty Athletic Hall of Fame, Class of 2008.

My wife, Vicki, and I met during spring training in 1979, and we were married in Little Rock, AR, later that year. I used my 90-day bonus money for her ring and a party. That night, we went to a waterpark and then a movie...Amityville Horror. We live in Seminole, FL, and a few miles from the Woodsman. Vicki and I have three sons, Ray, Jr., a carpenter; Ryan, who works in the tourism and hospitality business; and Robbie, who works in management.

(Ray Searage)

After graduating with my degree in education from West Liberty in 1977, I was the owner/operator of a Convenient Food Mart for 3-years. After that, I was hired to teach Physical Education in my hometown of Steubenville, OH. In 1984, I moved to Cambridge, OH, to teach PE at Cambridge High School, and to be an assistant wrestling coach with Jeff Carroll, who I knew from my wrestling days at West Liberty.

Two important things happened in my life in 1987. First, Coach Carroll left, and I was appointed head wrestling coach at the school. In the same year, I earned my master's degree in physical education from Ohio University. In 1990, I graduated with an administration degree from Salem International University (WV). In between all of this, I was the head football coach for five-years and the assistant baseball coach for three-years. One of my biggest joys in coaching was when one of my wrestlers won an Ohio state wrestling title. To this day, I still ask myself how I did all of this...coaching and earning two degrees...and still had time to fulfill my responsibilities as a teacher!

By the time I retired in 2015, I had risen to the position of assistant principal at Cambridge High School and had spent over half my life (35-years) in teaching and administration. Education is in my blood, and that's why I'm currently teaching PE at a rehabilitation center for adolescents. I have been married to my wife, Donna, for 38-years, and we have two adult children. Jason, who holds a degree in turf management, and works for professional golfer, Jason Day. Together, our son, Jason, and his wife, Hillary, have two children, Brandon and Lilly. Daughter, Kristin, an eighth-grade English teacher, and her husband, Seth, also have two children, Spencer and Dominic.

(Rick Spencer)

———

After leaving college, I went to work for Eastern Plating in Martins Ferry, where I became a Certified Welder. I was certified up to the Low-Pressure Boiler Certification. After 5-years of that, I decided to move to Florida mainly because of the trips we took as a Hilltopper baseball team.

This is where I started my first hotel job that went on to a 30-year career. I lived in West Palm Beach for 15-years, and this is where I met my wife. We married on September 4th, 1994, on the beach at Jupiter Beach Resort. Two years later, our first son was born, Jeremy, and when he was 3-months old, we moved to Independence, Missouri. This is where my wife was born and raised, and her family was still living. We moved in February, and it was 85 degrees when we left. When we got there, it was 13 degrees with an ice storm-- Welcome to the Midwest. However, this was the 2nd best decision I ever made next to first marrying my wife, Lisa.

With the move, Lisa had her job waiting for her, and I opted to be a stay at home dad. This lasted 6 months with me getting back into the Midwest hotel market. Twenty-three years later, I am still in the industry.

I currently coach at the college level in baseball with the Ban Johnson College Summer League. I have coached baseball for the last 20 years, along with coaching basketball for 8 years.

We own a Salon and Spa that my wife operates.

My oldest son, Jeremy, 24, played baseball in college and was a 4-year starter. Currently, he is a recruiter in the medical field. My youngest son, Jake, is a sophomore in college and plays baseball as well. He was a High School All-American, two-time All-State, Conference Player of the Year, two-time Examiner Player of the Year, and MVP of the Junior Sunbelt tournament that placed the top High School Juniors from around the country. I am an Ordained Minister with National Recognition. As a family, we are heavily involved in physical fitness. I am also a long time Ambassador with the Independence Chamber of Commerce.

(Tom Lufft)

When I left West Liberty, I went to work at Scio Pottery in Scio, OH. In November 1978, I left that job and began working for Sugardale Foods in Canton, OH. I retired from Sugarland Foods on March 2016 after 37-years. In 2015, I had the honor of being inducted into the Harrison County (OH) Hall of Fame as a three-sport athlete, baseball, basketball, and football. In 2018, I was inducted into the Tuscarawas County Hall of Fame.

I have been married to my wife, Linda, for fourteen years. Between us, we have four children, two girls and two boys. Our oldest is Jonne Jean, and next is her sister Brandi Nicole. The names of our boys are Zach and Cody. Linda and I also have nine grandchildren and one great-grandchild. We currently live in Louisville, OH.

(Jim Mellinger)

Between the last time I stepped off the baseball field in 1975 and now, a great deal has happened.

My coaching career came to a close in 1982 when I decided to hand the reigns of a highly successful baseball program over to Bo McConnaughy. During the eleven seasons leading up to that, my teams won over 150 games while losing less than fifty. From 1972 through 1982, my teams won ten WVIAC Northern Division Conference titles, five consecutive conference championships, and participated in Area 7 competition five times.

Although I was no longer coaching, I continued to be active at West Liberty, serving as Head Athletic Trainer and Associate Professor of Physical Education. My duties expanded when I was named Director of Athletics in 1989. One of my first achievements was providing leadership as the school move from being in the NAIA to NCAA Division II status in 1991. Six years later, in 1997, I was chosen to receive the Mike McLaughlin Award for my devotion and leadership to the conference.

In the decade that follows, I took an active role in the planning, design, and construction of the Academic, Sports, and Recreation Complex that opened during the 2000-01 academic calendar, the construction of the Outdoor Athletic Complex, which stands next to the ASRC, and the renovation of the baseball field and the tennis complex. The addition of women's soccer to the school's list of athletic programs in 2012 is also something I was very proud to have been a part of during my time as AD.

I was given the honor of being inducted into the West Liberty Athletic Hall of Fame in 2000. A few years later was chosen as the recipient of the NCAA Division II Southeast Region Athletic Director of the Year.

After forty-four years of service to the West Liberty community, over a quarter of a century as Director of

Athletics and eleven years as the head baseball coach, I retired in June 2015 to spend more time with my wife of 42-years, Lynn, and our three children. Matt, a manager in Chief Sports Book at Wheeling Island Casino; Brian, an Athletic Maintenance Specialist at West Liberty; and daughter, Jenna, who works as Life Safety Sales rep. for Johnson Controls in Pittsburgh.

(Coach Jim Watson)

My dad graduated from West Liberty in 1977 with a teaching degree in Math. He then went to work at #5 coal mine in Powhatan. The following year in June 1978, he married my mom. Before long, he returned to the love of his life…teaching Math classes at River High School in Hannibal, Ohio. These were not your basic math classes either. Dad taught the tough stuff: Algebra, Geometry, Calculus, and Trigonometry.

After teaching for a while, he decided he wanted to start a family, and teaching then just didn't pay enough, so he went to work at Ormet.

I was born on February 21, 1980. My dad's 25th birthday. I am pretty sure I was his best gift ever!

My dad continued his love for River High School students through tutoring. It was not uncommon for a student to be at our house at 5:00 or 6:00am sitting at the table as my dad helped them prepare for a test later that day. In between all of this, he continued to coach baseball at River and play baseball in the Coalminers League in Powhatan.

While being laid off at Ormet in 1985, he taught at Barnesville High School, where he was the Assistant Wrestling Coach and helped with baseball stats. Part of the way through the year, he was called back to work at the Ormet. During the day, he would teach at Barnesville and would leave straight from school to work the afternoon shift at Ormet.

Dad passed away suddenly on September 11, 1998, while keeping stats for the River High football team, also his alma mater, River High School. He was 43-years old.

In memory of his deep devotion, unwavering commitment, and endless love for everything River, the baseball field at the high school has since been named "Rick Bonar Field." My boys, Kaden and Kyler, got to throw out the first pitch on his field.

My mother, Susie, who has never gotten over her one true love, spends her time with her 3 new loves, her grandsons. My husband, Jim, and our three boys (my dad's favorite number, his baseball number), reside in Powhatan Point, Ohio. My dad would have definitely loved having three grandsons. Kayden (12), Kyler (8), and Koltyn (3), to spoil and teach. I continued to use the #3 tradition by using it as my volleyball and basketball numbers, and it has carried on with our sons using it as their sports number. By the way, Kayden, our oldest, is a talented pitcher and shortstop on a traveling baseball team…and all the boys love baseball. It must be in the genes.

Kristin Bonar Hunt, daughter
(*In Memoriam of Rick Bonar)*

Dr. Michael F. Price

The Final Out

"Life is like a baseball game.
When you think a fastball is coming,
you gotta be ready to hit the curve."
(Jaja Q)

I guess it's the minister coming out in me, but have often wondered *why* we twenty-four players on the '75 team were brought together at that particular point in our lives. Were we unknowingly predestined to be at West Liberty and were simply taking our place in some divine plan? If it was a divine plan, was it baseball and Coach Watson that brought us together and made us one?

Or, was it more serendipitous and by chance? Just as many of the other players might say that it was more by coincidence that the sons of truck drivers and steel mill workers, corporate accountants and lifelong criminals, and the sons of maintenance workers and convenience store owners, that these players found their way to the West Liberty campus that fall. Who would have ever believed that two players on opposite sides of the football field in the fall of 1971, one from Wheeling Central High School and one from Magnolia High School, would play on the same college baseball team four years later? Such was the case with Mike Anthony and Piney/the Woodsman. And speaking of the Woodsman, one of the teams on the 1973 Magnolia baseball schedule included the River High School baseball team…of which Rick Bonar was a member. The same goes for a baseball game between Steubenville High and Jewett High in the spring of 1971. Catching for Steubenville was Rick Spencer, and roaming the outfield for Jewett was Jon Kertes. Yet both would end up as teammates on the '75 Hilltopper baseball team. In turn, it was common for Kertes, and fellow

Jewett high alum, Jim Mellinger, to find themselves facing Ed Dulkoski from Cadiz High School in baseball every spring. And yet, all three would eventually make their way up Route 88 to the West Liberty campus. During his high school days at Weirton Madonna, Gregg DeSantis played baseball against Mark Stacy and Gary Freshwater. Fresh would play high school ball against Wheeling High product Robbie Schmidt and American Legion ball against Jon Kertes. Furthermore, it was not uncommon for another Wheeling High product, "T" Lufft, to regularly find himself playing opposite St. Clairsville, OH, player Shawn Girty and Donnie Hynes, or Oak Glen stand-out, Mark (Bear) Fabbro, who, in turn, most likely played baseball against Linsly products, Stan Duplaga and Paul Vargo. In the end, it seems that no less than twenty players on the '75 team report playing against one or more of their new teammates before coming to West Liberty.

One of the overarching themes of the movie *Forrest Gump* seems to ask this same question. Are the events in life pre-destined for us, or are these events happenstance? I am confident that the answer will be revealed to us in the future. If not during our time in this world, then for sure in the next. Consequently, maybe, just maybe, we should do as Forrest did and just let things happen and not ask why.

A more relevant question would be "how" 24 guys from various backgrounds in life were brought together in the autumn of 1974. There were guys on the team that came from a large city like Pittsburgh (PA); medium-sized cities like Deer Park (NY), Wheeling (WV), and Steubenville (OH); and from tiny towns like Jewett and Hannibal (OH), whose combined populations would hover around 1,000. How is it that they would end-up at West Liberty? To that, my friends, we know the answer. It was the game of baseball that brought Mouseyboy, Bear, Fresh, Frenchy, Girt, "T," Melby, the Woodsman, Spence, Stace, Harley, Zaugger, and the other eleven players together. More, it was baseball that played a significant role in transforming the lives of each of these two-dozen players that particular season of 1975 and beyond. These players can testify that lives were changed that year for the better, and forever, by baseball, either directly or indirectly. It was baseball that not only transformed each player on the team then but also had a major influence on the kind of individuals we players have become in adulthood. In many ways, it was baseball that brought us to West Liberty. It was baseball that kept us at West Liberty. It was baseball that played a major part in who we are today as human beings.

Willie Nelson was right: mommas should not let their babies grow up to be cowboys. Mommas should let their babies grow up playing baseball.

"Thank God for baseball."
(Mickey Mantle)

Dr. Michael Price
Largo, FL 2021